Endorsements for *Homosexu*

"This valuable book grapples with the core challenges faced by Christian families and churches as they encounter the vexing phenomenon of homosexuality. Yarhouse writes from a solidly biblical foundation, enriched with the best scientific findings of the day and wisdom gleaned from in-depth clinical experience with individuals, families, and churches. His new perspectives on the importance of sexual identity offer creative new insights helpful to Christians struggling with same-sex attraction."

—Stanton L. Jones, PhD, Provost, Wheaton College, and author of *Ex-Gays?* and the GOD'S DESIGN FOR SEX family sex education series

* * *

"Dr. Mark Yarhouse is a trustworthy voice for those who need to consider the complex issue of same-sex attraction. In *Homosexuality and the Christian*, he provides a clear and thoroughly readable resource that blends biblical understanding, empirical findings, and compassionate regard for the persons who ask these deeply personal questions. His wise answers lead the reader to the heart of the matter."

—Stephen P. Stratton, PhD, Professor of Counseling and Pastoral Care, Asbury Theological Seminary

* * *

"Compassionate, research-based, biblical, and practical, this is a sensitive and balanced overview of what we know about homosexuality and people who struggle with sexual identity issues. Dr. Yarhouse cuts through the myths and biases to combine the latest scientific research with real-life case histories and sensitive understanding of the various perspectives on this controversial topic. This is a must-read book for anyone who wants sound guidance and trustworthy information about homosexuality, including its relevance to Christians and the church."

—Gary R. Collins, Richmont Graduate University; School of Psychology and Counseling, Regent University

* * *

"*Homosexuality and the Christian* is the best book I have seen for evangelicals who want an accessible book that provides accurate, research-based information. Written from an evangelical perspective, the author is an authority on the topic of sexual identity and the Christian faith. This well-written book will benefit clergy, laymen, and policy makers alike. I highly recommend it."

—Warren Throckmorton, Associate Professor of Psychology at Grove City College, and Fellow for Psychology and Public Policy at the Center for Vision and Values

HOMOSEXUALITY AND THE CHRISTIAN

Mark A. Yarhouse, PsyD

BETHANYHOUSE

a division of Baker Publishing Group
Minneapolis, Minnesota

© 2010 Mark A. Yarhouse

Published by Bethany House Publishers
11400 Hampshire Avenue South
Bloomington, Minnesota 55438
www.bethanyhouse.com

Bethany House Publishers is a division of
Baker Publishing Group, Grand Rapids, Michigan

Printed in the United States of America

Library of Congress Cataloging-in-Publication Data
Yarhouse, Mark A.
    Homosexuality and the Christian : a guide for parents, pastors, and friends / Mark
A. Yarhouse.
        p. cm.
    Includes bibliographical references.
    Summary: "A leading Christian psychologist and researcher answers questions about
same-sex relationships and sexual identity with clarity and empathy"—Provided by
publisher
    ISBN 978-0-7642-0731-0 (pbk. : alk. paper)
    1. Homosexuality. 2. Homosexuality—Psychological aspects. 3. Homosexuality—
Religious aspects—Christianity. I. Title.
HQ76.25.Y37 2010
261.8'5766—dc22   2010015682

Cover design by Eric Walljasper

In keeping with biblical principles of creation stewardship, Baker Publishing Group advocates the responsible use of our natural resources. As a member of the Green Press Initiative, our company uses recycled paper when possible. The text paper of this book is comprised of 30% post-consumer waste.

15   16   17   18   19   20   21   13   12   11   10   9   8   7

To the local church:

May we be faithful witnesses who offer guidance and spiritual sustenance to those who are navigating sexual and religious identity concerns.

ABOUT THE AUTHOR

Mark A. Yarhouse is a professor of psychology and the Hughes Chair of Christian Thought in Mental Health Practice at Regent University, where he also directs the Institute for the Study of Sexual Identity (www. sexualidentityinstitute.org). Mark received BAs in philosophy and art from Calvin College, and MAs in theological studies and clinical psychology, and a PsyD in clinical psychology, from Wheaton College. Mark is an award-winning educator and scholar who has spent several years promoting dialogue between people who view the topic of sexual identity differently. In 2000, he chaired a groundbreaking symposium at the American Psychological Association's annual convention that brought together both gay psychologists and Christian psychologists to discuss common ground in treatment options for persons sorting out sexual and religious identity conflicts. He chaired similar symposia at the APA on the many meanings of marriage among different religions and various groups within the gay community; services for adolescents experiencing sexual identity confusion; and a new approach to working with sexual identity issues in counseling. Mark has written over fifty articles and book chapters and is the coauthor of several books, including *Modern Psychopathologies: A Comprehensive Christian Appraisal; Family Therapies: A Comprehensive Christian Appraisal;* and *Sexual Identity: A Guide to Living in the Time Between the Times.*

ACKNOWLEDGMENTS

People ask professors all the time about the courses they teach, what they write about, and what they research. When I answer, the conversation often either changes abruptly or is taken to another level. What I mean by this is that people either do not want to touch the topic with a ten-foot pole, or they want to share their two cents because they have really strong opinions. I want to acknowledge a few people who were willing to share their opinions with me, help expand my perspective, or otherwise challenge me on this difficult topic.

I have been blessed by the quality and longevity of conversations I have had with colleagues and students over the years. The School of Psychology and Counseling and the Doctoral Program in Clinical Psychology at Regent University have become stimulating schools and programs for the discussion of these and related topics. I am grateful for my colleagues here at Regent. In particular, William Hathaway, James Sells, Jennifer Ripley, Glen Moriarty, Judith Johnson, LaTrelle Jackson, Linda Baum, Lynn Olson, Vickey Maclin, Joseph Francis, Elizabeth Suarez, Cornelius Bekker, and Erica Tan have stimulated my thinking through ongoing discussions on this and related topics. Core team members and affiliates of the Institute for the Study of Sexual Identity (ISSI) have also played an important role in my thinking over the years, and there are far too many to acknowledge here. Current team members involved in ongoing discussions about sexual identity this past year include Audrey Atkinson, Katherine Chisholm, Kristina High, Robert Kay, Tiffany Erspamer, Camden Morgante, Heather Poma, and Alicia Tomasuno. Several ISSI team members served as readers of an earlier version of this book manuscript, including Jill Kays, Veronica Johnson, Trista Carr, Katie Maslowe, Heidi Jo Erickson, Heather Poma, Mary Zaher, and Deborah Mangum.

Colleagues, friends, and family also provided me with their comments and suggestions on an earlier draft, including Stanton Jones, Warren Throckmorton, Andrew Marin, Stephen Stratton, Janet Dean, Gary Strauss, Heather Sells, and Lori Yarhouse. Diane Cook helped edit portions of chapters 2, 8, and 9 for a DVD on sexual identity for young adults. I want to thank each of them for what they offered in terms of feedback to me, as well as the support and encouragement they have provided me over the years.

I need to also thank the people I have known both personally and professionally who have been sorting out sexual identity concerns. They have shaped my thinking about sexual identity through the relationships we have had, and I am especially grateful for the opportunity to know something about their lives and the decisions they have faced over the years.

MARK A. YARHOUSE
VIRGINIA BEACH, VIRGINIA

CONTENTS

Preface • 11

Part One: The Big Picture

1. What Does God Think About Homosexuality? • 17

2. Why Is Sexual Identity the Heart of the Matter? • 37

3. What Causes Homosexuality? • 57

4. Can Someone Change Sexual Orientation? • 81

Part Two: Honest Answers to Questions Facing Families

5. What If My Child or Teen Announces a Gay Identity? • 99

6. My Adult Child Announced a Gay Identity: What Now? • 119

7. What If My Spouse Announces a Gay Identity? • 137

Part Three: Questions for the Church

8. Whose People Are We Talking About? • 157

9. What Is the Church's Response to Enduring Conditions? • 177

10. Concluding Thoughts • 199

Resources • 219

Notes • 221

PREFACE

In a talk I gave recently at a Christian college campus, I asked the audience to "Raise your hand if you are nervous about listening to a conservative Christian speak on the topic of homosexuality." Several hands went up. While I was able to use that question to break the ice, it points to a real concern that faces the church today: Sexuality in general, and homosexuality in particular, are increasingly sensitive and divisive topics.

Some people are pushing hard for the church to change its teachings on homosexuality. Many mainline denominations are fracturing over the issue; people just don't want to hear anything that sounds like a compromise on a topic that has become something of a watershed issue for Christ and our culture. But these hot-button conversations are not just occurring within and across denominations; as our culture changes and as young people are coming into their own, these discussions are also taking place across generations. Many young people in the church, while theologically conservative, want to find new and creative ways to engage the topic in light of the relationships they have in their social circles.

This book is intended to be part of that discussion, and in some ways it is meant to help the conversation become more constructive. I think it can be helpful to move away from the well-worn path of discussing and debating the causes of sexual orientation and whether orientation can change. There is a place for an informed discussion about the causes of homosexuality and whether it can change; however, the overemphasis on those two points has left many people with far too few resources for navigating their sexual and religious identities. With apologies to Robert Frost, my focus is on the road less traveled: the intersection of sexual identity and religious identity. I encourage people to spend more time here, as I think sexual identity can be a neglected yet significant area for personal reflection, as well as a way to relate to others in a more constructive manner. It isn't so much about getting people into counseling so they can change; it's about equipping them to understand their attractions with reference to a larger sense of self and purpose. These things can be cultivated whether or not (or to whatever extent) orientation changes. Put differently, the cause of a homosexual orientation and the question of whether it can change, while meaningful topics in and of themselves, are secondary to the more pressing questions surrounding identity, sanctification, and stewardship.

I framed this book primarily around questions that people have asked me directly, as well as questions that point to what I believe to be important considerations. For example, a few years ago a young man asked me, "What does God think about homosexuality?" While it might not be the way I would phrase the question, it represents a concern facing many people who are sorting out this issue. Similar questions include "What causes homosexuality?" and "Can homosexuality change?" As I mentioned above, I am not convinced that these questions in particular are the most critical ones for the church today, but I understand they are important and that people want honest, informed answers.

Other questions get at what I think are important but often ignored issues, such as, "Why is sexual identity the heart of the matter?" The chapter that answers this question helps us take the discussion to another level. I want to demonstrate why I think shifting our focus away from orientation and toward identity can help us better understand what it means to be stewards of all we are, including our sexuality.

As the church wrestles with the topic of sexual identity and how to meet the needs of those who experience same-sex attraction, there are other questions that I think we should be asking ourselves, such as, "Whose people are we talking about?" and "What is our community response to enduring conditions?" The answers to these questions form a framework for providing counsel and pastoral care. The answers will also help us with how to deal with sexual identities within our families, so part 2 of the book answers several questions asked by family members: "What if my child or teen says he or she is gay?" "My adult child announced a gay identity: What now?" and "What if my spouse announces a gay identity?"

This book has been in the works for many years. In some respects it traces back to an invited address I gave at Calvin College years ago on sexual identity development among Christians. I remember that when I gave the talk, the person who was invited to respond to me thought I was going to lecture on how religious people are either not as likely to be homosexual or that they are unable to change orientation. So he talked about how religious people do have homosexual orientations, and he called into question whether people can willingly change sexual orientation. Both are valid discussions, but what he did not understand was that I was not talking about sexual orientation. Rather, I was talking about sexual *identity*—the act of labeling oneself based upon one's sexual attractions— and what influences it and how it develops over time. I was exploring the psychology involved in making meaning out of one's sexual attractions, and how that meaning could lead to labeling (or not), as well as the role of religious beliefs and values in that process. It was as though the other speaker and I were speaking past one another, and I have found that speaking past one another happens more often than not in discussions about homosexuality and sexual identity. This is partly because people are caught up in the familiar debates (e.g., what causes homosexuality and whether it can change) or are unable to step outside of the ways they normally think about this topic (discussing only orientation).

Please note that I open most of the chapters with a story out of my counseling practice or from consultations of which I have been a part. The people and their experiences are real, but the names and details have been changed to protect their identities.

This book is intended for a general Christian audience. I would like to see it help parents, pastors, and friends of fellow believers who experience same-sex attraction, and I anticipate that Christians sorting out these issues for themselves will find several of the chapters helpful too. It is a resource for the Christian community, some of whom experience same-sex attraction. We need new ways to think about this topic and the people who need support as they navigate a difficult path.

PART ONE
THE BIG PICTURE

CHAPTER ONE

What Does God Think About Homosexuality?

At the time, Scott stood out in my mind as a fairly unique teenager. His father brought him in for counseling because Scott had recently told him that he was attracted to other guys. Scott's dad shared this with his mom, and the two of them wanted Scott to "get help." I asked about Mom, but Scott's dad said she was working and wanted him to bring Scott in without her.

Scott's parents were Christians. When I asked how their faith related to their concerns, Scott's dad offered very little other than to say they did not think homosexuality would be a good idea for Scott. I wondered if Scott's father really thought that homosexuality was an "idea" that Scott came up with one day. But that discussion would have to wait.

Both of Scott's parents approached counseling for teenagers with the same mind-set: drop him off for help and pick him up in an hour. Neither of Scott's parents wanted to be involved in counseling, although I was able to convince Scott's dad to come in for a couple of consultations. This allowed me to get his perspective on Scott's concerns.

As it turned out, Scott's concerns were quite different from his parents'. Scott was not as interested in discussing his experiences of same-sex attraction. In fact, Scott wanted to talk more about theology than sexuality. He led off with the question, "What does God think about homosexuality?"

SOURCES OF AUTHORITY

This is not the ideal way I would frame the question, but it is what some people ask, particularly when they are Christians struggling with same-sex attractions. For other Christians, the answer has already been comfortably settled in their minds: They believe God does not condone homosexuality, or, at least, that He doesn't condone homosexual behavior. But an increasing number of people, Christians included, are asking this question for the first time. This is undoubtedly related to the broad social shift that has happened in which popular culture, entertainment, and the media have embraced homosexuality.

We must walk humbly around the question of what God thinks about anything. Not that we can't ultimately come to conclusions, but we need to be very careful in our approach. For one thing, when we try to answer this question, we don't want to lose sight of the person behind the experience. We will try to keep this in mind throughout this book.

In any case, as we think about this question, the first thing we need to decide is where we should go for the answer. Christians like Scott look to a number of sources of authority for guidance today, including (1) Scripture, (2) Christian tradition, (3) reason, and (4) personal experience.[1] All four of these sources are important to some extent, so let's look at each in turn.

Scripture

Christian doctrine affirms that the Bible is a reliable guide for the believer. Scripture is "fully truthful in all its teachings."[2] It is a "sure source of guidance"[3] in matters of faith and life, and although it is not a detailed textbook on human sexuality, it is a trustworthy guide in matters of sexuality and sexual behavior.

Rather than looking at Bible verses related only to homosexuality,[4] it is important to take a broader look at how God's Word deals with sexuality as a whole. A Christian understanding of sex is best understood through the four stages of redemptive history in the Bible: creation, the fall, redemption, and glorification. Each stage teaches us something unique about what God had in mind for our sexuality.

Creation. We begin with the creation story in Genesis 1 and 2. What are some things it teaches us about who we are as human beings, especially as it relates to our sexuality? First, we are completely dependent on God but also distinct from God.[5] Second, we are part of the creation. Third, human beings are placed in relationships; we are placed in families.

What is the nature of these family relationships? What we see in Genesis is that God created heterosexual marriage as the foundation of the family. This is affirmed later in the New Testament by Jesus, Paul, and others. God places the act of sex within the bounds of heterosexual marriage, and Christians should understand sex to be a good thing, something intended by God at creation.

Genesis affirms that God created two sexes, male and female, and that he wanted sexual intimacy to be kept within heterosexual unions. Creation is particularly important because it reveals what life was like before the effects of the fall. It was a state that God said was good, and therefore Christians should look at the creation story as having important implications for sexuality and sexual behavior. Through God's design and His stated pronouncements, Christians have understood that He is blessing monogamous, heterosexual unions.

We may go on from there to wonder why God placed human sexual expression in heterosexual marriage. There may be more than one answer to this question. First, sex in marriage is a "life-uniting act"[6] that is tied to transcendent, spiritual purposes. In other words, sex is more than just a physical activity, though it certainly involves the body. When Christians talk about how sex is tied to purposes that transcend it, they mean that it has a spiritual dimension to it that makes it bigger than the act itself. Sex is truly sacred. Therefore, sex outside of marriage violates what sex is meant to be—a life-union of man and woman.

Sex also has the potential to bring about new life. It's the natural way for a couple to "be fruitful and multiply," as we read about in Genesis. Of course not all sex in marriage brings about new life: some couples choose not to have children, and others are unable to have biological children because of infertility. But despite these exceptions, heterosexual sex is the means by which new life is formed, and the Bible places this way of forming new life in the specific relationship of heterosexual marriage.

There is also something that sex in heterosexual marriage can teach us if we look at it as a symbol of something bigger than the act itself. I mentioned above that sex is tied to transcendent purposes. In some ways our sexuality and the desire for completion in another reflects our yearning for transcendence, for something that is above or beyond the world we know. That alone is instructive. But we also learn in the Old Testament about the covenant, or promise, that God made with His people. God related to His people like a faithful husband to a wayward wife. He uses that image to convey something of how He feels when His people pursue other gods, when His people prefer idols. In the New Testament, Jesus Christ ushers in a new covenant. The husband-wife relationship is again used to illustrate the relation-ship between Jesus and the church, as the church is called the bride of Christ. For some reason God repeatedly uses marriage between a man and a woman as an object lesson; it tells us about God's love for His people—it tells us about Christ's love for the church.

However, sex is more than just life-uniting, or about procreation, or instructive, as important as each of those things are. It is also plea-surable, as we read about in other parts of Scripture.[7] It is something that couples take delight in. But again, in the Bible this is all in the context of the life-union between man and woman.

Think about eating for a moment. Having sex outside of heterosexual marriage is like the experience of eating for the pleasure alone. Although it is an imperfect analogy to sex, eating has many purposes. The primary reason for eating is to provide our bodies with the nutrients we need to survive. But eating is also instructive. Eating reminds us of our need for God, since it is God who provides our every need. Fasting has long been an important spiritual discipline. It reminds us of our dependence on God as our sustenance.

In addition to these useful purposes, eating can also be fun. But we are not supposed to just focus on foods that are pleasurable to eat. It is one thing to "Eat dessert first!" as the popular saying goes; it is another thing to eat only desserts. (The analogy breaks down, however—we need to eat to live, but we do not need to engage in sex to live, despite the fact that our sexuality and its expression is an important and meaningful part of human experience.) The point is this: We do not want to eat in a way that deprives food of its true purpose. Nor should we approach genital sexual activity in a way that deprives sex of its true purpose.

The fall. The idea of losing the transcendent purpose of food or sex is directly related to the fall. Because of the fall, we engage in behaviors in a way that disconnects them from their true meaning. The Bible states that all of creation has been tarnished by the fall. Evangelical Christians often emphasize individual sins—either doing the wrong thing or failing to do the right thing. But sin is also a state or condition. We are fallen, and we live in a world that is fallen. One author reflecting on the fall wrote that the world is "not the way it's supposed to be."[8]

Another author talks about sin as the "white noise" in the background.[9] Maybe you've seen white noise machines in a counselor's office, or perhaps you've used one to help you sleep at night. They emit a low noise that covers other noises, keeping people from hearing conversations or from being wakened by other sounds. Sin is like that. In fact, it is much more pervasive and far-reaching than that. It is the background noise of human existence. It's always on—so much so that we can adapt to it and forget it's even there. Sin affects human relationships and human sexuality. Again, this is not just about what we do or fail to do, but also how we see and understand the world around us. So the question is, what is the impact of the fall on sexuality?

At the individual level, "being fallen" is probably best understood as a splitting of the will.[10] In Romans 7, Paul talks about his own internal struggle with obedience and disobedience to God. This reflects a divided will, and in the area of sexuality, this divide is very clear. Many people struggle with obeying God's revealed will for sexuality and sexual behavior.

The fall has affected sexuality in many ways that have little to do with homosexuality, and there are a large number of examples of this throughout Scripture. For instance, in the New Testament scene in which Jesus was asked about divorce, He noted that although divorce is allowed in the Old Testament, it is not God's best for people; it isn't God's heart. Also, according to the Bible, sexual behaviors and relationships that occur outside of marriage (such as sex prior to marriage or adultery) are sinful. Additionally, sex that is demeaning, whether within marriage or outside of marriage, is a result of the fall and is not considered God's intention for sexuality. Probably the most common effect of the fall that we struggle with today is our tendency to turn people into objects. As a society we have the sinful capacity to fragment others, to think about humans as interchangeable objects for personal sexual gratification.[11] This is a growing problem with our easy access to such images through the Internet and magazines.

And finally, as important and meaningful as relationships can be between two people of the same sex, sexual behavior between them is considered one of many things that fall outside of God's revealed will.

Christians tend to focus on the sins of others, including sexual sins, while overlooking or discounting their own struggle with sin.

But many Christians are beginning to realize that homosexuality is one of those areas that can get a disproportionate amount of attention while other areas of concern, such as greed, envy, or pride, remain largely unchecked.[12]

Redemption. Christians understand that God in His mercy did not leave us in our sin. He did not abandon us to our fallen state. Rather, God had a plan for the redemption of a chosen people and of the broader creation. Redemption was set in motion immediately after the fall, but it came to a culmination with the birth, life, death, and resurrection of Jesus. That said, the victory that believers experience in Christ is not yet complete. Indeed, Christians live in the "in between times," as one theologian put it.[13] We are in the "now" and the "not yet" of the victory we have in Christ. In other words, we live a life that is redeemed and set apart for God's purposes, but not all has been made perfect.

God uses certain relationships and institutions to protect us and to foster in us the qualities that are important to Him. For example, the church can be thought of as an institution that God established to provide for us and to protect us. A healthy church is a blessing that helps equip the believer. Similarly, there are ways in which marriage can be seen as providential. Marriage is the relationship God identifies as reflecting the many purposes of sexuality and full sexual expression. So it is a place for sex to be "life-uniting" (or at least to have that potential); it is a place that offers us the instructional aspect of what God says to us about His relationship with His people; and it is a place for us to enjoy and delight in the physical pleasure of sex.

Sex outside of marriage does not reflect God's intention for sexual behavior, but a person's experience of sex outside of marriage may not be different from that of sex within marriage. In other words, Christians cannot deny that there are meaningful relationships, including same-sex relationships, that are formed and maintained outside of heterosexual marriage. Sex outside of marriage may be pleasurable or even produce children. But this does not mean that these are the kind of relationships God intended for full expression.

Christians affirm that we are in a place in history in which Jesus has secured the victory on the cross, but that victory is yet to be completed. This is the time of redemption, and God uses us to further the cause of redemption in our own lives each day.

Glorification. The story of creation, the fall, and redemption comes to a culmination with the return of Jesus. This is referred to as "glorification," the last major act of redemptive history. So how does glorification affect how we view sexuality?

Glorification confirms that the church is our "first family"[14] and that biological ties should not be our top priority on this side of heaven. Our primary identity is a Christian, and we must look at everything else we are in light of this fact.

> The church is God's most important institution on earth. The church is the social agent that most significantly shapes and forms the character of Christians. And the church is the primary vehicle of God's grace and salvation for a waiting, desperate world.[15]

Do you remember when Jesus was asked about what marriage would be like in heaven? It was a trick question—people were trying to get Him to comment on a theological debate that was going on at the time. But Jesus didn't bite. He said that there would not be giving and taking of husbands and wives in heaven. Should we assume, then, that there will be no marriage in heaven? No, that's not quite right. You see, although marriage will not exist between two human beings, marriage will exist between the church, the bride of Christ, and Jesus, the Bridegroom.

This should give us some insight into our sexuality today. Keeping glorification in mind helps us understand the place of our sexuality and its expression. Sexuality is important for a number of reasons, but it is not our first identity. Our primary identity is that we are part of a body of believers who are wed to Christ. This is true whether we are single or married. Each of us is part of the bride.

The church is not only considered the "primary vehicle of God's grace"; it also represents the believer's main identity as a Christian, a follower of Christ. This can be discouraging when the church falls short of its potential in important areas, including how we as a community respond to fellow believers who are sorting out sexual identity questions. On the other hand, it can also be inspiring when we catch a vision for who we could be in relation to those who are struggling among us and in our communities.

Glorification, then, reminds us of what we, as individuals and as a body of believers, are moving toward. God's concern is to help us grow into the fullness of our potential.

To summarize what we have covered so far, sex in heterosexual marriage is affirmed by the Bible for three primary reasons. First, it is a symbol of our relationship with the Lord. This was conveyed in metaphors throughout the Old Testament between God and Israel, and in the New Testament between Christ and the church. Second, sex in marriage is good because of the unity it creates between one man and one woman. Third, sex in marriage is good because it is the sole means of procreation, even when procreation is not chosen or not possible due to other issues such as infertility.

According to the Scriptures, sex outside of a heterosexual union falls outside of God's will and intention for us. This is not limited to homosexual sex, but it does include it. Despite the reinterpretations some theologians have attempted, it seems clear that Scripture speaks with one voice on the topic of homosexual behavior. Let's now turn our attention to Christian tradition.

Christian Tradition

Scripture forms the basis for Christian tradition. Indeed, Christian tradition is not about believers discovering new truths about their faith; it is about passing on truths to the next generation and addressing current issues in light of one's faith. It involves being faithful to what those who went before us understood to be true in terms of the person and work of Christ. How has Christian tradition understood homosexuality?

When considering homosexuality and Christian tradition, we need to acknowledge that there are a lot of different beliefs represented within the Christian faith. We can't cover the whole spectrum in a book of this size, but let me briefly review Roman Catholic and Protestant stances.

Roman Catholic Christianity.[16] Roman Catholicism has traditionally been shaped by the Church's interpretation of the Scriptures and historical traditions. According to the Catechism of the Catholic Church, a summary of the official teachings of Roman Catholicism, the purpose of marriage includes the good of the spouses as well as the procreation and education of children.[17] Historically, more emphasis has been placed on procreation; more recently, however, there has been an emphasis on the relationship of husband and wife as a covenant that symbolizes the love Christ has for the church.[18]

In the twelfth century, marriage was recognized as a sacrament by the Catholic Church; it was formally accepted at the Council of Florence (1439) and the Council of Trent (1545–1563).[19] Marriage as sacrament meant that the marriage ceremony was a "principal means by which God communicates the grace (favor) that heals human beings of sin and elevates them into the divine life."[20] The Catholic Church holds that a "married life that begins in this context has the overtones of a shared commitment to journey ever more deeply into the mysteries of salvation."[21]

What does this understanding of marriage have to do with a Catholic view of homosexuality? The Catholic Church does recognize homosexuality as a real sexual orientation, meaning that it is an enduring pattern of sexual and emotional attraction. (This is in contrast to some Christians who see heterosexuality as the only real sexual orientation, with homosexuality being more like an addiction or other concern.) But in spite of this view, the Catholic Church holds that same-sex behavior is against natural law and that homosexuality itself goês against God's original design for sex.

A Roman Catholic view also takes seriously the fact that same-sex relationships do not allow for procreation. Same-sex relationships cannot reflect the various meanings of marriage found within Catholicism. Therefore, the person who experiences same-sex attraction is called upon to live a chaste life, accepting their same-sex attractions as a personal trial in their walk with God.[22]

Protestant Christianity. Despite the diversity of denominations represented within Protestantism, the majority express similar views on sexuality and marriage because they share a common history in the Continental and English Reformation movements.[23] The relationship between husband and wife is viewed as a "covenantal bond." This covenant symbolizes the relationship between God and His people that is conveyed in the Old Testament (e.g., Jeremiah 3:14), or the relationship between Christ and the church as presented in the New Testament (e.g., Ephesians 5:22–33).[24]

One modern trend among Protestants has been to decrease the emphasis on procreation within marriage in order to take a more companionship-oriented stance;[25] therefore, one of the primary purposes of marriage in Protestant Christianity is the love and companionship between husband and wife. Having children has become secondary and an outflow of the marriage relationship.[26] Some view this companionship trend as a more secular, modern, and Western phenomenon, and believe that conservative Protestant Christians still emphasize the importance of procreation, or at least the potential to procreate, as it relates to marriage within a heterosexual union.

Protestant tradition sees sex within the context of marriage as a normal and positive product of humanity's creation as male and female.[27] In other words, sex is good and proper in the context of heterosexual marriage, but only in that context. Protestant Christianity values celibacy but tends to show a preference for marriage.[28] This preference is not true in Catholicism.

Those within the Protestant Church who oppose this traditional stance on sexuality and marriage are primarily coming from mainline denominations rather than conservative or evangelical ones. Since the early 1970s, many mainline churches began debating the morality of same-sex behavior and whether to bless same-sex unions. There certainly has been a historical consensus—a Christian tradition—but that is being challenged in many Protestant denominations today. This challenge seems to reflect broader issues, with many of the challengers questioning the authority of Scripture and opposing a theology that recognizes the potential value in redemptive suffering. But in spite of these challenges, most Protestant denominations still do not bless same-sex unions or ordain practicing homosexuals.

Some Protestant groups have moved toward a stance similar to that of Roman Catholicism, holding that if people cannot change their sexual orientation, they are called to live a chaste life in keeping with traditional interpretations of Scripture and Christian tradition.[29] In other words, their stance is that there is no sin in individuals being same-sex attracted, as long as they abstain from homosexual acts.

So there is a traditional Christian sexual ethic seen in both Roman Catholic and Protestant Christianity. That ethic is grounded in Scripture and has been held throughout the history of the church. It would be a radical departure from church tradition for Christians to embrace same-sex behavior and relationships today. Those Christians who are making this shift seem to be doing so based on reason and personal experience rather than the teachings of Scripture or church tradition.

Reason

When people cite "reason" as a source of authority, they are typically thinking of scientific advances that have furthered our understanding of homosexuality. In a different book, a coauthor and I discussed the relevance of science to the church's moral debate.[30] We identified several ways in which people have tried to move the debate about homosexuality away from the church's traditional sexual ethic.

The major areas we discussed were: (a) the commonness of homosexuality; (b) the causes of homosexuality; (c) whether it is a mental health issue; and (d) whether sexual orientation can change from homosexual to heterosexual. Here are a few quotes from people who have tried to use science to move the church away from the traditional sexual ethic in some of these areas:

- *Commonness of homosexuality*: "If the best scientific data . . . seems to put the figure of gay and lesbian people in the world at about 10 percent of the population . . . then you and I need to realize that 10 percent is such a large percentage that it could hardly be accidental."[31]

- *Mental health issue*: "If it could be shown that homosexuality is generally a symptom of unmet emotional needs or difficulties in social adjustment, then this might point to problems in relating to God and other persons. But if that cannot generally be shown, homosexuality may be compatible with life in grace. . . . The scientific evidence is sufficient to support the contention that homosexuality is not pathological or otherwise an inversion, developmental failure, or deviant form of life as such, but is rather a human variant, one that can be healthy and whole."[32]

- *Cause of sexual attractions*: "If organic or body-chemical explanations should, however, prevail, we are reminded . . . how this would make even more indefensible moral condemnation of same-sex preference or assertions of its unnaturalness."[32]

In chapters 3 and 4 I will review some of the research that is being used to support these bold claims. But for now I'll just say that the science is often poorly understood, it's overstated, and it is essentially misused by those who are attempting to change the church's historical teaching about sexuality and sexual ethics.

The best studies suggest that only 2 to 3 percent of the population is homosexually oriented, but to some extent those numbers shouldn't affect a Christian stance either way. At least as far as behavior is concerned, many patterns of sin are common, such as pride, while others are rare, like cannibalism. The point is, whether something is common or rare is a separate issue from whether it is wrong.

When we look at the causes of homosexuality, we simply do not know why some people experience same-sex attractions or have a homosexual orientation. There are probably many factors that contribute in one way or another, with these factors varying from person to person. In the final analysis, does the cause of same-sex attraction fundamentally change the Christian sexual ethic? No. We are all called to live the way that God reveals is good for us in terms of sexuality and sexual behavior.

There was a definite shift thirty to forty years ago in which mental health professional organizations declared that homosexuality was no longer a mental disorder, and we've seen more recent attempts to portray it as a healthy expression of sexual diversity. But there is mixed evidence for the truth of this claim, and the fact that our culture has shifted is not fundamentally central to the Christian sexual ethic. In other words, the question of whether something is defined as a mental disorder has very little to do with whether or not it is a sin. Many patterns are deemed "mental disorders" but are not sinful patterns of behavior, such as schizophrenia. On the other hand, many sinful patterns of behavior are not "mental disorders" but are sinful behaviors or attitudes, such as greed.

Finally, there has been an ongoing debate about whether people can change their attractions or orientations. When we look at this debate, we need to realize that this also is not directly relevant to the moral issue. The Christian should focus on being faithful to God's revealed will, and for most Christians the concern is with behavior rather than attractions or orientation. Changing sexual orientation is one thing. Changing behavior is another.

So these are the common arguments from reason or science. They are often cited as grounds for moving the church down a certain path—away from the conclusions drawn from reading Scripture and from Christian tradition.

Personal Experience

One final source of authority that is brought into the debate about homosexuality is personal experience. It is important to listen to fellow believers who experience same-sex attraction. Gay Christians have an important perspective to offer, but we should also listen to the voices of sexual minorities who do not form a gay identity, by which I mean those Christians who are attracted to the same sex but decide not to act on these attractions or form a gay identity based upon these attractions. These people seem to be disparaged by people on both sides of the debate.

Perhaps the reason many conservative Christians won't listen to them is because certain segments of the church have made very strong claims that people who are attracted to the same sex can be healed or completely changed. They think that if a person has enough faith they can change their sexual orientation to the point that they are attracted to people of the opposite sex. This could lead some same-sex attracted Christians to feel the pressure to claim that they've been "cured" and are completely changed, even if they aren't. This added pressure should be lifted, and the experience of those who attempt change and who have benefited from it, even if they haven't changed completely, should be explored and better understood.

On the other side of the spectrum, many Christian communities have emerging groups supporting a gay identity. We see this in the Roman Catholic Church: The group Dignity, although not an official Roman Catholic group,[33] was developed with this purpose in mind. Similar groups have emerged in nearly every Protestant mainline denomination today.

Gay Christians tend to emphasize that their homosexuality is "who they are." They can no more remove that from their overall sense of identity than can African-American Christians remove being black from their identity. In our studies of gay Christians, a common theme was that of authenticity—gay Christians told us that it would be inauthentic to deny their own homosexuality. One woman we interviewed talked about her experiences that confirmed her sense of identity as a gay Christian: "Confirmation came for me when . . . I found happiness or contentment . . . being with a woman. . . . Every time I chose to do what was natural, it felt like confirmation."

It is important to recognize that sexuality should be experienced as central to a person's overall sense of identity. I think this was intended by God. We are inherently physical beings, and we are inherently sexual beings. So we don't want to communicate that our sexuality is somehow removed from who we are.

On the other hand, it is also important to recognize that when we ask what God thinks about homosexuality, we are likely to confuse the pattern of behavior with the person. In other words, while we can acknowledge that some gay Christians say behavior and identity cannot be separated, other Christians who experience same-sex attraction do precisely that. They separate behavior and identity, seeing it as a necessary step in navigating their sexuality in light of their faith. When we instead ask what God thinks about homosexually oriented people, or what he thinks of people who experience same-sex attraction, we can answer without hesitation that God loves them. And as Christians we should take the lead in demonstrating the love of God in real, sustained relationships.

When we are asked as a church to listen to the voices of sexual minorities, I think it is important that we do just that. We want to avoid, however, listening only to those who have chosen to embrace a gay identity. As I mentioned above, we do well to also listen to those who have chosen not to integrate their sexual attractions into their behavior. Their personal experiences contrast with those who embrace a gay identity. It isn't that those who do not identify as gay deny their attraction to the same sex; rather, they choose not to form an identity around their attractions. In the studies we have conducted, they tend to form an identity around other aspects of who they are. For example, one person shared the following:

> My faith in Jesus has allowed Him into my life to heal wounded
> areas. With healing comes strength and maturity—which
> enabled me to grow up and out of the [same-sex attraction].
> And if I do have fleeting moments of [same-sex attraction]—I

remember why it happened, and I think of God and who I am in Him. I can let go of the attraction and move on and be at peace.[34]

As we discussed in seeing sexuality in light of glorification, some Christians foster a primary identity as part of a larger body of believers who share with one another an identity in Christ.

Their experiences, taken together with the proper role of science and an understanding of Christian tradition and biblical revelation, speak an important message to sexual minorities today. That message is a message of meaning and purpose that is found in God's provision and in stewarding one's sexuality and sexual identity. There are those who are attempting to live out the Christian sexual ethic as understood from Scripture and Christian tradition, and their voices, their personal experiences, must also be heard by the church today.

WHAT SOURCES OF AUTHORITY DO YOU EMPHASIZE?

I've been reviewing the four major sources of authority that people in the church turn to for direction on the difficult topic of homosexuality. But, of course, most people don't treat these four sources as equally authoritative. Each of us places greater relative weight on some than others. It is important to reflect on what weight you give to each of them, as well as the weight others are giving to these various sources of important information.

Some Christians claim to give greater weight to personal experience and reason. But what I think they are actually doing is giving greater weight to the experiences of those Christians who have embraced a gay identity. Meanwhile, they don't seem to be as open to the personal experiences of those Christian sexual minorities who have chosen not to embrace a gay identity. These same Christians also appear to favor a certain reading of science. They apply that understanding of science to the moral debate in the church, and by doing so they believe the findings make Scripture and Christian tradition less relevant.

This then makes them question Scripture and Christian tradition, which can lead to some interesting efforts to reinterpret Scripture to fit a shift in beliefs and values that they have brought to the Word. This is understandable; it can be difficult to grapple with Scripture when someone you are close to, someone you know and love, such as a daughter or son, is struggling through these issues. Or perhaps they are not struggling but rather feel greater expressed happiness or contentment as a gay person in a same-sex relationship.

Other Christians appear to give greater weight to Scripture and Christian tradition. This is good, although I hope that all four sources of authority are given consideration. For them, Scripture is "trump," and the weight of Christian tradition is substantial too. They can pay attention to the findings from science without believing that science is able to settle the moral debate for the church. After all, science describes what occurs and can be measured; it doesn't tell us how we ought to live or why we should choose one behavior over another. In other words, this group of Christians recognizes the limits of science on ethical decision-making. If they do listen to Christian sexual minorities, they tend to listen to those Christians who do not form a gay identity. They may value that aspect of personal experience but are suspicious of those who identify as gay and Christian, seeing them as championing a cause—a change in sexual ethics that goes against Scripture and Christian tradition.

CONCLUSION

"What does God think about homosexuality?" Scott asked. It's an important question to a sixteen-year-old who takes his faith seriously. It's also an important question to those who love Scott and others like him.

At the time Scott's question seemed unique, particularly for a teenager, but I see more and more young people asking it these days. Unfortunately, the question blurs the distinction between the person and their actions. People who experience same-sex attraction or have a homosexual orientation may or may not engage in same-sex behavior.

Such behavior is a concern to the Christian because of what we believe God intends for sexuality and its expression.

So what, then, should be our answer to this question? Although we could look at the specific passages of Scripture that address homosexuality directly, many Christians find it more helpful to look at the Scriptures in their entirety. In the end, the Bible speaks with one voice on the matter. When we add the weight of Scripture to the weight of Christian tradition; when we look carefully at the relevance of scientific research on matters of sexual ethics (science is able to describe what *occurs in nature* but not *how we ought to live*); and finally, when we reflect on the personal experiences of sexual minorities who integrate their attractions into a gay identity *and* those who choose not to because of their effort to live in conformity to God's revealed will, the evidence points to a traditional understanding of how God sees homosexuality. In other words, our conclusion is that homosexual behavior is not appropriate for the Christ-follower.

As for the person, the sexual minority, God loves them. And, just as with any other person, God desires a relationship with them.

So Christians will want to be careful and humble in their attempt to answer the question of what God thinks about homosexuality. At the same time, there is a tremendous cultural push to change Christian ethics and church teaching on the morality of same-sex behavior. In that sense, the question is being asked more frequently than ever, and there is a need to answer with doctrinal clarity in the context of pastoral care and respect. In all matters, including our sexuality, it may be helpful to talk about being good stewards of what we have been given. We will discuss this further in subsequent chapters.

But there is also a pastoral piece to this discussion. I don't think God is sitting at a distance seeing what people will do with the circumstances they are in. I think God is very active in our lives, identifying with us in our longings and struggles, including attraction to the same sex and the desire to experience full sexual intimacy. And I think the Christian can invite God into that experience of longing—the Christian can invite God to speak to him or her in that desire. The

French writer Paul Claudel once said, "Jesus Christ did not come to take away suffering from the world. He did not even come to explain it. He came to fill suffering with his nearness."

This language will sound foreign to our ears. Our culture today emphasizes personal fulfillment and individual attainment—not what it means to conform our lives to the Word of God. Although it contrasts sharply with a Western culture that focuses on felt needs and "self-actualization," Christians are called to say no to some experiences so that we can say yes to a life that is obedient to God's revealed will. Our understanding of that revealed will is found in Scripture, witnessed to in Christian tradition, illuminated by science properly conducted and interpreted, and confirmed by the lives of those who are living faithfully before God. Indeed, from Christian sexual minorities we learn that the Christian life is one in which we become more Christlike rather than just fulfilling our potential. Or, to put it more accurately, our potential can only be truly fulfilled in obedience to God and His claim on our lives, including our sexuality and its expression.

TAKE-HOME POINTS

- Avoid proof-texting from Scripture.

- A biblical understanding of sexuality and sexual behavior should reflect the four acts of the biblical drama: creation, the fall, redemption, and glorification.

- There are four general sources of authority: Scripture, Christian tradition, reason (science), and personal experience.

- Personal experience should include both those who want to change the church's teachings on homosexuality and those who live in conformity to God's revealed will for sexuality and sexual behavior.

- Everyone favors one or two sources of authority over others— it can be helpful to reflect on which sources of authority you favor and why.

CHAPTER TWO

Why Is Sexual Identity the Heart of the Matter?

So here's what I'd like you to do, God helping you: Take your
everyday, ordinary life . . . and place it before God as an offering.
Embracing what God does for you is the best thing you can do
for him. Don't become so well-adjusted to your culture that you
fit into it without even thinking. Instead, fix your attention on
God. You'll be changed from the inside out.

—ROMANS 12:1–2 (THE MESSAGE)

The apostle Paul tells us not to "become so well-adjusted to your
culture that you fit into it without even thinking." One way that
we, as followers of Christ, have not followed this teaching is in the
language and categories we use to discuss and debate homosexuality.
We've allowed our culture to choose the terms of the debate.

And there are casualties.

Both liberals and conservatives focus too much energy on the cause
of homosexuality. Both sides presume that if they win the battle, it
will settle the moral debate. Liberal voices often argue for a biological
(nature) basis of homosexuality, claiming that if biology is the cause,

then we cannot hold those who have a homosexual orientation to the traditional Christian sexual ethic. Conservatives, on the other hand, often argue for environmental (nurture) causes, which emphasize personal responsibility and the claim that people can change their orientation. Both liberals and conservatives make their arguments as if the gospel hinged on these claims.

I have a question for you: Can we set this aside? We can come back to it later. But for now, can we focus our attention on something else? I want to consider the end point: sexual identity.

When I was in grade school, one of my favorite pastimes was solving puzzles and mazes. One way I approached mazes was to find the end point and work my way backward. I found that knowing where I was headed helped guide my decisions along the way. This ultimately helped me complete the maze much more quickly and with fewer wrong turns. In fact, that's a common strategy in successfully navigating any tricky path in life—see where you're headed and work backward from the end point. So that is what we are going to do in this chapter as we focus on sexual identity.

Understanding sexual identity is crucial for the church right now. In fact, the concepts I will introduce in this chapter may be ground-breaking for many readers as they think about the issue of homo-sexuality. My goal here is to do nothing less than change the entire conversation. And to some extent, much of the rest of this book will hinge on what we will discuss in this chapter.

WHAT IS SEXUAL IDENTITY?

You may have been so busy arguing about what causes homosexual-ity and whether or not it can change that you never thought of talking about identity at all. After all, aren't sexual orientation and sexual identity the same thing? Actually, they are not. The simple answer is that sexual identity is how you label yourself by your sexual prefer-ences. Common sexual identity labels include straight, gay, lesbian, and bisexual. Others include queer, questioning, and bi-curious.

Public sexual identity is how you identify your sexual preferences to other people or how other people label you, whereas *private* sexual identity is how you identify your sexual preferences to yourself. These identities can be the same, or they can be different. A person could be known publicly as gay or bi and think of themselves in those terms. On the other hand, a person could have a public sexual identity as straight while privately thinking of themselves as gay.

Most people understand what is meant when someone says they're gay, straight, or bi. They're using language that conveys something to other people about their sexual preferences. That's what we call sexual identity.

So sexual identity is about labels. But the sources of a person's identity can be complicated. What might influence a person to use one label over another? Here is a list of some things that could contribute to one's identities. This isn't a formal list. It's just something I put together based on my research and clinical experiences. Keep in mind that these influences are weighted differently for different people.

- Your *sexual attractions*
- Whether you were born *male* or *female*
- How *masculine* or *feminine* you feel
- What you *intend* to do with the attractions you have
- What you *actually do* with the attractions you have
- Your *beliefs* and *values* about your sexual attractions and behaviors

Think about what might contribute to how you would label yourself publicly and privately. What pressures or expectations could play a role? For example, being male or female might be a contributing factor, so we could say that biological sex matters in terms of sexual identity. Also, how masculine or feminine you feel is related to social norms—what others tell you are masculine or feminine behaviors or attributes. Sexual attractions also matter—for example, you may be attracted to the same sex, the opposite sex, both sexes, or neither.

But it isn't only about how you feel. Your actions matter too. Being attracted to someone and acting on those attractions are two separate things. And if you are like most people, your intentions and your behavior can sometimes be in conflict. What you actually do with your attractions can be part of your identity, but not necessarily. Have I confused you yet?

And what about your beliefs and values? How will they play into your identity? This question, of course, brings us into a Christian context. Religious beliefs and values, like everything else, are weighted differently for different people.

Let me illustrate the weight of some of these factors with two examples. I remember meeting two men in about a week's time who helped me understand how people identify various aspects of themselves differently. One young man experienced a pretty strong same-sex attraction. He identified himself as gay and Christian. We talked about the way different things might impact identity and labeling. He shared that his values and his same-sex attractions were "trump" for him, outweighing everything else. He believed God made him gay and that he was fine identifying publicly and privately as gay. He had strong same-sex attractions and, although he had not yet engaged in same-sex behavior, he had no questions or concerns about doing so. Based on the relative weights he put on the different aspects of himself, he identified himself as gay.

Later that week I met with another young man who also experienced strong same-sex attraction. Interestingly, he did not identify as gay. We talked about the way different things might impact identity and labeling, and he shared that his values and behavior were the most important things to him. His values were that he affirmed a traditional Christian sexual ethic, and this made an impact on his behavior. He had not engaged in same-sex behavior because of these values. In fact, he felt that God wanted him to pursue a life of chastity, and he was at peace with that. His primary identity was as a believer (or "in

Christ") rather than his experiences of same-sex attraction. In other words, based on the relative weight of the different aspects of himself, he focused on his faith identity over his sexual attractions.

So both young men experienced strong attraction to the same sex. Neither had yet engaged in same-sex behavior, but they each had very different opinions about doing so. As we can see from these two examples, many factors may contribute to and form a person's decisions about a public or private identity. For one person the feelings of same-sex attraction may be weighted more heavily. For another person, religious beliefs might play a larger role. For yet another, it all comes down to the actions they've taken. How you identify yourself is a decision based on any number of factors working in numerous and complicated ways.

So how should we think about sexual identity as it relates to sexual orientation?

A THREE-TIER DISTINCTION

When talking about homosexuality, I think it is helpful to make a three-tier distinction between attractions, orientation, and identity. No, they are not the same thing.

The first tier is *same-sex attraction*. Using this term is the most descriptive way people can talk about their feelings. This is the part of the equation they can't control. Certain people, regardless of the cause, have experiences of attraction to the same sex. This fact doesn't say anything about either their identity or their behavior. It doesn't hint at who they are or what they do. It is descriptive. We are simply talking about the fact that a person experiences same-sex attraction.

The next tier is *homosexual orientation*. When people talk about having a homosexual orientation, they are essentially saying that they experience a same-sex attraction that is strong enough, durable enough, and persistent enough for them to feel that they are *oriented* toward the same sex. If it is *only* toward the same sex, they might say that they have a homosexual orientation, whereas if it is toward both sexes they might say they have a bisexual orientation. The person is simply describing the amount and persistence of their own attraction, which is based on what they perceive attraction to be. That may seem like a subtle difference, but it is an important one to consider, because one's perception of attraction may be on target or it may be skewed.

No one knows how much attraction to the same sex is necessary for a person to feel that their orientation is now homosexual or bisexual. This would be impossible to measure. We do know that some people experience some same-sex attraction but are completely comfortable saying that their sexual orientation is still heterosexual. We take this to mean that the attractions to the same sex are either not particularly strong, are fleeting, or are limited to a specific person.

The third level, *gay identity,* is the most prescriptive. It is a socio-cultural label that people use to describe themselves, and it is a label that is imbued with meaning in our culture. Did you realize that throughout history, only contemporary Western culture has used the self-defining *gay* attribution? Although homosexual behavior has been practiced in other cultures throughout history, we are the first culture in which people refer to themselves in this way. There was never a language for it, and there has never been community support for this kind of identification or labeling. Until recently, there was not even a way to say it. Talking about a gay identity is part of a modern, contemporary movement. When people take on this label, they move beyond describing their experience and instead are forming their identity. When most people talk about "being gay," they are usually revealing more than their attraction to the same sex; rather, "being gay" has taken on certain connotations—perhaps some would say it has taken on a life of its own.

Here's another way to look at the three-tier distinction: The vast majority of people have opposite-sex attractions. About 6 percent of men and 4.5 percent of women report[1] feeling attracted to members of the same sex. But only about 2 percent of men and about 1 percent of women apparently have strong enough same-sex attractions that they would say they have a homosexual orientation. Then, presumably, some percentage of those with a homosexual orientation have integrated their attractions and orientation into a gay identity. I don't know what percentage that is because researchers do not typically tease that out.[2] They might ask about attractions, they might ask about orientation, but they usually don't ask about an identity. Often we presume they are the same thing—we collapse the three tiers into one so that the person experiencing same-sex attraction is presumed to be gay.

I explained this to Todd one day. Todd is a young man in his mid-twenties, and I was meeting with him about sexual identity concerns he had. What he said about the three-tier distinction was that it was something many of his acquaintances in the gay community would not fully understand; they might feel it was "splitting hairs" to make the distinctions. However, he said it was tremendously helpful to him in that it provided him with the "intellectual space" he needed to sort out his own sense of sexual identity. It created just enough room for him to be able to ask and answer questions about what his attractions meant to him, how they fit into his overall sense of identity, and how they might relate to his personal faith as a follower of Christ.

What I want to recommend is that we keep the three tiers distinct and try to be more descriptive. For those who find it helpful, we can create and keep open this "intellectual space" for them to sort out their own sense of identity. Talking to people in specific terms about their attractions is more helpful than presuming that an identity has already been shaped around these attractions.

Interestingly, in the 1970s the average age of labeling oneself as gay was twenty years old. Today the average is about fifteen.[3] To the gay community, this is seen as an improvement. They believe it is a good thing for a young person to know who they are at an earlier age. Perhaps they themselves wished they could have been more open about their identity at a younger age. In any case, they believe that early disclosure and labeling will keep young people from being closeted or from questioning who they are. Social conservatives, on the other hand, are generally alarmed by these findings. They are concerned that fifteen is too young to commit to an identity label.

WHEN AND HOW DOES SEXUAL IDENTITY OCCUR?

Sexual identity labeling does not happen all in one day; it is usually a slow and difficult process. The first question we need to ask is, What leads young people to question their sexual identities in the first place? Although it isn't the same for everyone, research indicates that for girls, an attraction to same-sex friends plays a significant role in labeling. Another factor is exposure to the topic of same-sex attraction in the classroom, in movies, and in other forms of entertainment. Girls more often than boys tend to explore this possibility in existing relationships—which usually means a current friendship or a dating relationship with another girl.[4] As one researcher summarized these findings: "Overall, females are more likely than males to have stable same-sex relationships, to have few sex partners, and to attach emotional, romantic meaning to their same-sex relationships before engaging in sexual behavior."[5]

Boys also talk about how their attraction to the same sex is a part of questioning their identity, but often same-sex behavior plays a bigger role than it does for girls. A boy's first same-sex behavior is more likely to occur in a "purely sexual encounter" with another male.[6]

In other words, same-sex sexual identity in women usually happens when a girl realizes she is attracted to a female friend, whereas same-sex identity in men often happens following purely sexual encounters.

The people who participate in these studies are typically found in community centers or community support organizations that are specifically designed for youth who already identify as gay. Personally, I do not think this represents all young people who experience same-sex attraction. But from what we know from these and other studies, females tend to have a more positive attitude about their attractions and identity than males;[7] their experience with labels may be different, however. Females may be more likely to experience their sexuality and their sexual identity as fluid.

As I mentioned above, sexual identity doesn't just turn on or off— it emerges through a developmental process. It begins typically with attraction, and then it leads to a behavior of some kind. So it often starts with same-sex attraction and then moves into same-sex behavior. This may then lead to a questioning of identity, which results in the act of self-labeling. Some studies suggest that it takes about three to four years for females to go through the attraction, behavior, questioning, and labeling cycle, and five to six years for males.[8] Admittedly, most of this research has been done on males.

Of course these are just averages. It can take as long as fifteen years in some studies to go from this initial attraction to labeling.[9] From the research I have done, for Christians it can take even longer.[10] I think this has to do with the weight Christians give to their faith commitment as it relates to the identity and attraction issues. Some churchgoers are in heavy conflict about their sexual identity because a lot is at stake for them (in many cases, for instance, their church relationships could be in jeopardy). They take their time to unpack these issues. The question is not resolved quickly, or even in a couple of years.

Sexual identity development appears to begin with sexual attraction from as young as age ten or twelve, and then perhaps moves on to same-sex behaviors by around thirteen to fourteen. By age fourteen, questioning of identity may occur, followed by labeling at around age fifteen.[11]

What is happening developmentally throughout this process? During the teen years, kids try on different roles and eventually consolidate an identity. This is a critical developmental task for them. There have been a number of gay scholars who have offered up models, or theories, of how sexual identity develops. If you were to study this area in a human sexuality class, your teacher might reference a model proposed by Vivian Cass.[12] Her model begins with identity confusion. A person is confused by experiences, feeling different from his or her peers because of attractions to the same sex. Then the realization of difference becomes a tolerance of the possibility that "I am homosexual."

Next, as the individual's homosexuality develops, there is an acceptance that "this is my identity." With the swinging of the pendulum toward identity comes the conclusion that all things homosexual are good and all things heterosexual are questionable. Then the pendulum swings back to the center. The person incorporates their identity into a larger sense of who they are in the world.

That is a classic model, but there have been others suggested as well. When the initial models of homosexual identity development were introduced, they tended to treat males and females as essentially the same. It was all too common for psychologists to focus research on men and then simply apply it to women. Lesbians understandably felt that drawing general conclusions about the gay community based on research done mostly on males was misleading. Eventually models were developed that distinguished between lesbian sexual identity and gay male sexual identity. But then bisexuals within the gay community pointed out that their experiences were different from both gay male and lesbian experiences, so additional models were proposed. Ethnic minorities who were same-sex attracted also noted differences in their experiences from what was being accounted for by all of the previous models. So they developed and proposed models of their own.

Where am I headed with all these distinctions in sexual identity models? Well, there seems to be yet another group missing from this research. What about people who are same-sex attracted but do not embrace a gay identity? These people are often alienated from the gay community and the organizations that support them. Since the standard outcome of most models is that same-sex attracted people achieve a gay, lesbian, or bisexual identity, what about those who do not?

Generally, researchers agree that young people who experience same-sex attraction will find themselves going through three stages:

1. There is an *identity dilemma*; in other words, something is different from what other people are experiencing.
2. There is *identity development*. This is the whole process of sorting out sexual identity and what attraction to the same sex means. A person going through sexual identity development is asking

questions like: What do same-sex feelings signal about me? How do I make meaning out of these attractions? Are they at the core of who I am as a person? Are they one part of me, but not the main part of my identity?

People may reevaluate the answers to these questions throughout their lives. Because of this, there is some fluidity when it comes to an individual's identity. Not everyone stays on one course. People make different decisions at different stages in their lives about how they identify themselves.

3. Finally, they get to a place of *identity synthesis,* or the sense that the person feels they've "arrived" at their identity or sense of who they are. They find themselves satisfied with their identity and talk comfortably about it. This last status is being questioned by some studies that suggest that an end point may be less important than leaving sexuality more "open-ended" in terms of labeling. However, most researchers still think of synthesis or achievement as a reasonable goal people move toward.

As we touched on earlier, recent research suggests that identity labels change over time, particularly among women. In one study that began over ten years ago with eighty-nine women who experienced same-sex attraction, it was the norm for the women to experience both attraction to the same sex and attraction to the opposite sex. In other words, these women were not exclusively attracted to other women. And most changed their identity label throughout their lives, with 21 percent of the women switching their identity label to "heterosexual." Also, many (37 percent) preferred not to label themselves at all.[13]

Others[14] who study sexual identity see similar trends among youth. They see the term *gay* as more ambiguous than ever before as fewer and fewer teens who experience same-sex attraction are choosing to label themselves at all.

Sexual identity is a developmental process; how a person approaches their identity dilemma and what happens next in terms of identity development is so important as he or she tries to get to synthesis, or an end point of identity. The key, as we'll discuss next, is the way a young person responds to what can be referred to as the "gay script."

THE GAY SCRIPT

When I use the term "script," I'm referring to a way in which we come to understand ourselves and our lives. Scripts reflect the expectations of our culture in terms of how we are supposed to live and how we should relate and behave. We have scripts around so much of human experience, including expectations for relating to the opposite sex and to the same sex, as well as decisions about when to "settle down" and get married, when to have children, how to relate to one another in marriage, and so on.

Scripts also extend into the world of expectations we have for our sexuality and how we experience and express ourselves. Scripts can then extend into discussions about sexual identity. In our culture today, experiences of same-sex attraction are typically treated as synonymous with a gay identity, and a gay identity carries with it many connotations; e.g., if you are attracted to the same sex, then you are gay. However, being gay means not only are you attracted to the same sex, but you are personally fulfilled through engagement in same-sex behavior. The three-tier distinction we made earlier just collapsed in on itself.

To understand what I'm going to say about scripts, it is important to understand how scripts function in the lives of actors. Actors read from scripts all the time. They use scripts to determine how their character thinks and feels and relates to others. Young people similarly look for scripts to read from to make sense of who they are. And young people who experience same-sex attraction similarly look for a script to read from.

Let's imagine a sixteen-year-old named Chris. He experiences same-sex attraction and is looking for resources to inform him about who he is and what his experiences are all about. Let's imagine that Chris is like an actor on a stage. He is looking for instructions or guidance on how to relate to the audience. Chris is looking for a script.

When it comes to treating the experience of same-sex attractions as one and the same as having a gay identity, much of the gay community is ready to hand Chris a "gay" script. Here's what I think this script looks like:

- Same-sex attractions signal a naturally occurring or "intended by God" distinction between homosexuality, heterosexuality, and bisexuality.

- Same-sex attractions are the way you know who you "really are" as a person (emphasis on *discovery*).

- Same-sex attractions are at the core of who you are as a person.

- Same-sex behavior is an extension of that core.

- Self-actualization (behavior that matches who you "really are") of your sexual identity is crucial for your fulfillment.

This is a compelling script. The confusing attractions that Chris experiences are seen as natural and intended and blessed by God, placing a great emphasis on the sexual diversity seen in nature. They give way to discovery. They allow Chris to learn about who he really is. The attractions are central to his sense of himself as a person. This script tells Chris that no one can question or judge his behavior because same-sex behavior is merely an expression of his central identity. Finally, in our culture today, a culture that emphasizes "self-actualization" (realization of a person's potential) and is saturated in messages about the pleasures of sex, Chris receives the message that he has every right to act according to his sexual identity.

If you were in Chris's shoes, I think you would be drawn to this kind of script. Notice the emphasis on discovery as the primary metaphor in the gay script. A young person discovers who he or she already is. The young person is categorically different from other young people by virtue of his or her attractions to the same sex.

The question is, what other options are even made available to Chris and other sexual minorities? What competing or alternative script can he expect from the church? When Chris looks to the church he hears very little, and what he does hear is usually an oversimplification of the causes of homosexuality, followed by the claim that it can easily be changed or healed through efforts or faith. Is this the only message the church wants to send Chris?

I was once presenting this idea of a gay script to a group of Christian leaders. They resonated with the claim that same-sex attraction is often treated as synonymous with a gay identity, and that all of this is packaged in a script that young people choose because they have no other options. During the Q & A time one leader asked me: What is the alternative script? What do young people read from if they do not read from the gay script? What *else* do they have available to them?

At that time, I did not have an alternative to offer. I thought that it should emerge from the voices of those sexual minorities who do not adopt the gay script but instead develop a different one. Since that time I've had the opportunity to hear from people who have read from a different script, and I now believe I see one of possibly many alternative scripts emerging.

ANOTHER SCRIPT FOR CHRISTIANS: IDENTITY "IN CHRIST"

Many Christians have chosen not to let their attractions determine their identity. For example, we recently conducted a study of Christian college students who experience same-sex attraction.[15] They shared with us some of what they experienced on their college campus and how their identity developed over time. It was interesting to us that very few of them adopted a gay identity. They appeared to have another way of seeing or experiencing their attractions to the same sex. Many attributed their attractions to the fall, for example, as something that wasn't God's intention or God's ideal for sexuality or sexual behavior.

In another set of studies[16] we compared Christians who adopted a gay identity label to Christians who chose not to adopt a gay identity label. Both groups experienced same-sex attraction. Both groups identified themselves as Christians. We found that both groups were interested in living in a way that was consistent with their beliefs and values. But they had two very different ways of doing this. The Christians who adopted a gay identity made their beliefs and values line up with their identity and behavior. In other words, identity and behavior came first, and their beliefs and values had to be adjusted to them. On the other hand, the Christians who did not adopt a gay identity made their identity and behavior line up with their beliefs and values. For this group, beliefs and values came first.

The Christians who adopted a gay identity talked about worshiping God as gay Christians—that doing so was what it meant to be authentic before God. In contrast, the Christians who did not adopt a gay identity indicated that authenticity meant worshiping God on God's terms. Worshiping God out of a gay identity would not reflect true authenticity to them.

The message that has emerged from these studies is that of another script (and there may be many others). It is essentially an "identity in Christ" script that stands in sharp contrast to the gay script. Here are the script's[17] basic points:

- Same-sex attraction does *not* signal a categorical distinction among types of person, but is one of many human experiences that are "not the way it's supposed to be."[18]

- Same-sex attractions may be part of your experience, but they are not the defining element of your identity.

- You can choose to integrate your experiences of attraction to the same sex into a gay identity.

- On the other hand, you can choose to center your identity around other aspects of your experience, including your biological sex, gender identity, and so on.

- The most compelling aspect of personhood for the Christian is one's identity in Christ, a central and defining aspect of what it means to be a follower of Jesus.

This script relies on the metaphor of *integration* rather than *discovery*. Remember that the discovery metaphor assumes that the attractions tell us who the person "really is." The integration metaphor, on the other hand, begins with a description of the attractions to the same sex and then recognizes that a young person has choices to make about both behavior and identity. The young person can integrate his or her attractions into a gay identity or not.

A young person can then go on to center their sense of identity around other aspects of themselves as a person. Perhaps the most central theme we hear among those who choose not to identify as gay is that they form their identity around the person and work of Jesus Christ. Rather than focus on an identity that is a negative (*not* gay), they form an identity that is "in Christ," a positive sense of themselves and their sense of purpose and community that is based on the redemptive work of Christ in their own lives.

I also want to point out that some Christians who experience same-sex attraction adopt a gay identity but *transform the meaning of the word* gay. That is, they use *gay* to simply mean that they experience same-sex attraction or have a homosexual orientation. In other words, they use *gay* as a kind of shorthand that is readily acknowledged in the broader culture.

Let me illustrate this with a specific example. Rob understood the three-tier distinction but decided it was just easier for him to begin his interactions with others by acknowledging that he was gay. He said he felt like he was being honest with them about his attractions by using common terms that are familiar to others. To him, there was freedom in that. Some people distanced themselves from him because of this, particularly people in his local church, while others simply accepted this as the starting point in getting to know him. People often assumed he engaged in same-sex behavior because they associated that with "being gay." But as they got to know him, he was able to share with them his decision to pursue chastity. Nevertheless he preferred to call himself *gay* as his starting point rather than begin by trying to explain the nuances found in using more descriptive language.[19]

I think this is a trend that will continue. I believe that more

Christians who experience same-sex attractions, particularly young people, may find that the word *gay* functions as their shorthand for what they experience in terms of attractions. The challenge they will face is the challenge the young man faced above: some people will find that label difficult to respond to, in part because the current connotations surrounding it have to do with endorsing same-sex behavior. This may change too; we will have to see how it impacts the decisions young people make about labeling. Of course, others will continue to find the word *gay* problematic for many reasons, and they will prefer to not identify with the word given its current connotations. As I have been suggesting throughout this chapter, they will form an identity around other aspects of who they are as a person, particularly if they feel that their identity can be formed around the person and work of Christ.

FINAL THOUGHTS ON SEXUAL IDENTITY

A few years ago I came across an essay[20] on how people form a political identity. It was really about how people come to experience their political views as central to who they are as a person. It talked about the stories people live by and how these stories come to shape them. The author teased out two major threads of these stories: *ethnic* and *civic* aspects of identity. *Ethnic* aspects are unchosen aspects of identity, while *civic* aspects of identity are voluntary agreements with certain people or groups that support that identity. He was trying to explain that people can choose to join communities and eventually experience that community as intrinsic to who they really are.

Do you see the connection to sexual identity? Same-sex attraction may be the ethnic aspect of identity, an unchosen characteristic that can contribute in some way to identity, but there are also civic aspects of identity, and people have choices to make regarding what they believe about sexuality, sexual identity, and sexual behavior. These choices will lead them to different communities that, in turn, confirm and consolidate a sense of this sexual identity into who they are.

Dallas Willard, in his discussion of the Beatitudes and the kingdom of God, wrote that "We were made to 'have dominion' within appropriate domains of reality. . . . Our 'kingdom' is simply the range of our effective will. Whatever we genuinely have the say over is in our kingdom."[21] In other words, God gives us control over certain aspects of our lives.

I remember interviewing one woman who experienced same-sex attraction. She was part of a study of Christian identity and sexual identity labeling. She spoke about how the church labeled people, including her, and what that did to her sense of the options that were in front of her: "The church's influence was to be quick to put labels on people. I took them for myself. Homosexual or not. There were no options at times, and I felt very stuck in that."

A man in the same study shared something about identity too:

> The Holy Spirit started working on my life and initiated in
> my life. My friends who were Christian loved me. I came to
> the Lord . . . because it made sense. I didn't come to Christ to
> escape homosexuality. The Lord reminded me of a verse . . . one
> day. . . . That day, God interrupted my prayer. He revealed to me
> His love. His word showed me that He is loving enough to tell
> me something isn't good that turned my identity around. I knew
> I couldn't be the same after that prayer time.

Did the man go on to experience a change in his sexual orientation? Not that I recall. Rather, his change had to do with identity rather than orientation. A change in his identity and how he thought of himself before God was an important step; it provided an inroad to tremendous spiritual growth and maturity, quite apart from whether or not his orientation changed.

If we as a church continue to believe that deep spiritual maturity can only come with a change in orientation, then we will be waiting forever for those people who are trying to change but can't. Either that or we will place great pressure on them to say that they have experienced dramatic change even when they have not.

What the church can help people with—regardless of whether

orientation changes—is identity. We can recognize that a gay script is compelling to those who struggle with same-sex attraction, especially when they see few options emerging from their community of faith. Therefore we can help develop alternative scripts that are anchored in biblical truth and centered in the person and work of Christ. We can also look at our own lives and whether we are really prepared to live in a way that makes Christ our primary identity, whether we experience same-sex attraction or not.

TAKE-HOME POINTS

- Many people have found it helpful to make a three-tier distinction between same-sex attraction, a homosexual orientation, and a gay identity.

- Sexual identity development can be thought of in three broad stages: identity *dilemma,* identity *development,* and identity *synthesis.*

- Sexual identity development begins with sexual attraction at as young an age as ten or twelve, and may involve same-sex behaviors around ages thirteen or fourteen; this may be followed by a questioning of identity and, for some, identity labeling at around age fifteen.

- The "gay script" makes use of the *discovery* metaphor by emphasizing that same-sex attractions signal who a person really is, making categorical distinctions among types of people based on sexual attractions.

- An alternative script focuses on the metaphor of *integration* and whether a person integrates same-sex attractions into a gay identity.

CHAPTER THREE

What Causes Homosexuality?

Rick looked like a typical sixteen-year-old kid. He was listening to his MP3 player in the waiting room when I called his name. His parents looked up and shook his arm, and they all walked back to my office for our consultation.

His parents had called two weeks before and expressed concern because Rick had recently admitted he was gay. His mother had asked him about it when she found out that his best friend was gay. She said she suspected it about his friend, but not about Rick. She shared the news with her husband that night after dinner, and he was said to have been "surprised" and "disappointed," but in general he was quiet and didn't have a lot to say then . . . or now. Rick's mother, on the other hand, had a lot to say. She was concerned about him; she was angry too. She didn't understand how it could be true. She started to share examples of girls Rick had dated at the beginning of high school and as recently as last year.

"What about that dance last year?" she asked, not really waiting for an answer. "What about that girl you went to the dance with?

She was cute. You said you liked her. Was that for our benefit? Was that a lie?"

Rick tried to answer. "It wasn't a lie. It wasn't for you or for anyone. I liked her just fine, but I don't know. All I can tell you is what I feel now. You asked me, and I told you. If you didn't want to know, you shouldn't have asked."

Rick's mother turned to me. "What caused this? Is he really gay? Is this a choice he's making, because it feels like a choice. It feels like a bad choice too, and sometimes I just want to shake him and tell him to stop it!"

At the start of the next session, Rick's mother apologized for getting so upset in the first meeting. "I'm sorry I got so loud last time. This whole thing has me upset. I'm confused. I'm frustrated. I'm not sure what to say. . . ."

"But I've been wondering," she went on, "was it something we did? Or was it something we didn't do?"

Rick spoke up. "Mom, it wasn't anything you or Dad did. It's not like that. Tell her, would you?" Rick looked at me.

QUESTIONS THAT MATTER TO FAMILIES TODAY

If you are reading this book, you may have asked similar questions. You might sympathize with these parents as they try to find answers. Perhaps, like them, you are thinking in terms of choice: Did my son or daughter choose this? How did he or she come to make this choice? What about the values we've been trying to instill for years? What about his or her dating history—doesn't that mean that this gay identity is a sham?

From there you may wonder if there is something you did or didn't do that contributed to your son's or daughter's experiences of same-sex attraction. *What did I do wrong? Was I over-involved emotionally? Did I not care enough? Did I care too much?*

On the other hand, you might be reading this book and sympathizing with Rick. Maybe you are sorting out questions about sexual identity and are looking for answers. Maybe you want to communicate clearly to your parents that it isn't a matter of finding fault. You want to protect them from negative messages that place blame on them, as if they did something that directly caused your same-sex attractions.

This book was written to shed more light on an area that is often difficult to see clearly. Sometimes this can be done by providing much needed information, but there will be other times when we will gain clarity by learning what we *don't know*, recognizing that more insight and understanding might not be available just yet.

The question "What causes homosexuality?" is one of those areas where recognizing what we know and don't know is likely to be the best we can do right now. When I first launched the Institute for the Study of Sexual Identity (ISSI) in 2004, I contacted our university IT staff about setting up an institute Web site. We were working out the design and layout of the various Web pages when the IT person suggested I offer a FAQ page for Frequently Asked Questions.

Although I had not given it much thought, when I considered a FAQ page, the first question that came to mind was likely the first thing most people ask when they talk to a counselor about homosexuality: What causes homosexuality? The answer: We don't know. It was going to be a pretty short Web page.

Actually, we could spend a fair amount of time explaining exactly what it is we don't know about the causes of homosexuality. You might keep that in mind as we venture into this chapter.

AN AWKWARD QUESTION FOR THE CHURCH

The focus today on causes of homosexuality has gotten the church into an unfortunate position. Many Christians are perceived by our broader culture as either ignorant about science or anti-science. Part of this perception probably comes from the fact that when the subject of homosexuality comes up, many Christians talk about choices people make, and they appear to give little or no credence to the biological hypothesis. I've met some Christians who say that people choose homosexuality. I don't know if they literally mean that a person gets into their late teens or early twenties and selects homosexuality from among a host of options, realizing that it might be stigmatizing, socially isolating, devastating to their parents, and so on. I doubt Christians actually think people choose it like they choose a major in college, but they are often perceived that way. At the same time, some Christians say things that make you wonder if that isn't exactly what they mean.

What's happening is that many in the church are polarized against the gay community on all things related to homosexuality. In the nature vs nurture debate, if the gay community says nature, the church will say nurture. And that is exactly where we are today. Although I disagree with those in the gay community who advance the conclusion that nature is the sole cause of homosexuality, I also disagree with Christians who take the position that it is all nurture. Both groups are most likely wrong. They are committing the sin of *nothing-but-ism*, as one of my former professors used to say. The sin of nothing-but-ism is proclaiming that some experience or condition is caused by nothing but _____ (add your pet theory here, e.g., abuse, childhood abandonment, etc.).

People in the Christian community and people in the gay community can both be guilty of committing the sin of nothing-but-ism. But instead of seeing how unhelpful the debate is, both groups get a lot of mileage out of advancing their position.

And there is a cost to the Christian community.

Do you remember the thought exercise we did in the last chapter? We imagined Chris as a teenager who was on a stage looking for a script to make sense of who he was, what he was experiencing, and how to relate to others.

Rick is in a similar situation to Chris. Rick is looking to the church and to the gay community for information and resources. But when Rick looks to the church he finds that the church is staying entrenched in the position that homosexuality is not in any way caused by nature, which goes directly against what some of the most outspoken members of the gay community are saying. The church's position is as much defined in opposition to the gay community as anything else. Rick hears from them that homosexuality is caused by parent-child relationships.

In addition to emphasizing environmental causes of homosexuality, the church talks about homosexuality as sin, often even presenting it as the worst possible sin.

Rick turns to the other side of the stage and sees the gay community. The gay community says that homosexuality is natural; it is a normal part of human experience, a celebration of the range of sexualities people can experience, and one that doesn't have to be defended. Which do you think a young person is going to find compelling? To a young person who experiences same-sex attraction, who feels confused and alone, the message from the gay community will likely be much more comforting and attractive.

I want you to keep Rick in mind. We will return to him and his family. He represents so many young people who are asking good questions about their sexual attractions and sexual identity. And they are looking for resources. They are looking for information. The church has an opportunity to speak into people's lives, but we need to think through our message. What is it we are trying to say? For now, remember Rick as we discuss the possible causes of homosexuality. Remember that he is trying to make sense of how his sexual attractions fit into the "role" he is to play in his church and in society.

Equifinality

As we begin to look at the possible causes of a homosexual orientation, I want to introduce you to the concept of *equifinality*. What this means is that there are multiple pathways to a given end point. Have you ever gone to MapQuest or used GPS to get directions for a cross-country trip?

I was recently driving across the state of Michigan with my dad and sister. We had put our destination into the GPS system, but then we found ourselves in a traffic jam on one of the major highways.

We decided to turn around and find another way. Unfortunately, the GPS had a one-track mind, and it kept "recalculating" and directing us back to the traffic jam. "Turn here! Turn here!" it would proclaim in an attempt to get us to where it knew we wanted to go. (Of course, turning "here" would have put us across another lane of traffic or into dense woods or in someone's field.) It struggled to process what we knew immediately: that there were many ways to get from where we were to where we wanted to go.

Let's extend the analogy with MapQuest. If you put in your starting address and your ending address, you will receive step-by-step instructions (that are mostly correct) on how to get from here to there. (I find that they lose a little of the details right at your destination, but that's a topic for another day.) While we receive one specific path for going from here to there, we can recognize that there are actually many ways to get from here to there. We can take major highways or we can take back roads. We can take tunnels and bridges, or we can try to avoid them altogether. We can take the most direct route, or we can take a scenic route. We can stop to see great sights, such as the nation's largest ball of string, or we can pass that by entirely.

This illustrates the point of equifinality: There are many ways to an end point. The same principle we see in cross-country trips can be seen in homosexuality; that is, there are multiple pathways to a particular person experiencing same-sex attraction or a homosexual orientation. No one pathway captures every person's experience.

I would add one other important insight into homosexuality: I don't think there is one end point either. This is where our analogy to traveling across country might break down. There may be many ways to get from Washington, D.C., to San Diego, CA, but there is only one San Diego, CA. I suppose the better analogy would be if we were going from the East Coast to the West Coast. We could say that there are many ways to get there, and we could also say that there are many different experiences of the West Coast. There are differences between Northern California and Southern California, not to mention the range of experiences in specific cities across the state and in other states along the West Coast, such as Oregon or Washington.

With homosexuality, the end point suggests to me that we are really talking about "multiple homosexualities," if you will. I think most people would agree that male homosexuality seems different from female homosexuality. But I think we also see differences among men. There is no one male homosexual experience; rather, different men experience homosexuality differently. The same is true for women. There is not one female homosexual experience. Because of this, as we discuss some of what we know and do not know about homosexuality, we want to keep in mind that the end point of a homosexual orientation can probably be reached through different pathways, and that these pathways ultimately suggest different experiences of homosexuality—hence multiple homosexualities.

WHAT COULD CONTRIBUTE TO HOMOSEXUALITY?

When I think of the possible influences on homosexuality, I think of four broad categories. Each person probably experiences and responds to the factors in these categories differently, and there may be other categories worth exploring, but I think these four capture the main possible causes people discuss today.

The main contributing factors are found in: (1) biology, (2) childhood experiences, (3) environmental influences, and (4) adult experiences.[1] Let's briefly summarize what we know and do not know in each of these four areas, recognizing that they may be weighted differently for different people.

Biology

We noted earlier that there are many explanations being investigated that fall under the umbrella of "the biological hypothesis." The biological hypothesis is that biology plays a substantive role in the development of homosexuality for most persons who experience same-sex attraction or who say they have a homosexual orientation.

The popular understanding of how biology plays a role, however, is that it is the same as the role it plays in eye color or hair color. In other words, if a gene says you have a homosexual orientation, then you have a homosexual orientation. But that is not what homosexuality is like. We will want to return to this, as it may be why so many Christians refuse to even consider biology as playing any role whatsoever.

Research is conducted to advance the biological hypothesis on many fronts. Scientists have investigated adult hormonal levels, prenatal hormonal levels, direct genetic studies of chromosomal markers, twin studies, birth order studies, animal model studies, finger length ratio studies, and so on.

Although I will not be able to discuss all of the studies that have been conducted to advance the biological hypothesis, I'd like to discuss a few that have received more than their fair amount of attention. I will treat these as examples to illustrate some of the benefits and drawbacks of the research in this area.

Also, I face a dilemma in discussing this research. It is tempting to jump in and throw around words like *interstitial nucleus of the anterior hypothalamus* and *midsagittal plane of the anterior commissure*, but I think most people's eyes would glaze over pretty quickly. So rather than do that, I am going to explain the main points and concerns in normal, everyday language, and then offer the relevant references for those of you who want to learn these words and start dropping them into your conversations at the next church picnic.

Areas of the brain. Various regions of the brain are studied to test the biological hypothesis and, specifically, the prenatal hormonal hypothesis. In other words, the theory that hormones during pregnancy can cause homosexuality. Certain regions of the brain, if they are different between heterosexuals and homosexuals, might suggest differences due to exposure to certain hormones prenatally. One well-known researcher[2] conducted just such a study in the early 1990s. He reported that the hypothalamus region of the brain was larger in heterosexual males and females than it was in the homosexual males he studied. Researchers were later able to confirm differences between the male and female hypothalamus, but they have not been able to confirm differences related to sexual orientation. The original study was criticized by many researchers for having a small number of participants and for studying an area of the brain that can change under different circumstances, such as if a person is on a certain medication. Critics also pointed out that even if these differences were to be reported by other researchers, it is unclear if these differences are the *cause* of homosexuality or the *result* of homosexuality. After all, we know that behavior can influence various regions of the brain too, so we don't want to assume that the differences in size automatically mean that they play a role in causing homosexuality; if real differences exist, they could also be the result of behavior or other environmental influences.

Twin studies. Another highly influential line of research has been conducted on twins. These are commonly referred to as "twin studies." Although many researchers have studied identical twins in which one or both twins had a homosexual orientation, the most significant study was published in the early 1990s and continues to be cited in many textbooks today.

The researchers[3] who studied twins in which one of the twins was homosexual reported higher concordance rates among identical twins than among fraternal twins or other siblings. *Concordance rate* is a fancy way of saying how likely one thing is to occur when something else occurs. In this case, the researchers were wondering about the likelihood of one identical twin being homosexual if the other twin is homosexual; or one fraternal twin being homosexual if the other is homosexual; or one sibling (not a twin) being homosexual if the other sibling is homosexual.

Keep in mind that identical twins are formed from one egg and one sperm; they are always the same sex and they always have the same eye color. Fraternal twins, on the other hand, are formed from two eggs; they are as genetically similar as any siblings born to the same parents.

In any case, the researchers reported a higher than anticipated concordance rate for identical twins. It was higher for them than for fraternal twins or nontwin brothers.[4] However, the criticism of the study was that the researchers had gathered their sample of twins from ads placed in pro-gay magazines, which could have biased the study toward such a high concordance. When the researchers later published a study[5] using a better sample of twins who were more randomly selected, the concordance rate fell by more than half of what it was in the first study.

What does this mean? It means that these studies do not provide much evidence to support the biological hypothesis. The hypothesis may be true, but it does not have these twin studies to lean on if it is to find support. More recent twin studies[6] share many of the same concerns as the original one we've been discussing.

On the other hand, one of the largest and most recent twin studies[7] does provide us with some interesting information. It is the largest twin study of homosexuality conducted to date. According to the study, the genetic (biological) contribution to homosexuality was rather modest and lower than expected by those who are certain that it is all biological. What was much more significant were other experiences that are *not* shared by twins. In other words, *unique* or *novel experiences* by individuals accounted for more of what contributed to homosexuality.

So this twin study tells us a lot by telling us very little about any one particular theory, whether that favored theory is genetic (the so-called "gay gene") or environmental (strained parent-child relationships). The evidence is just not conclusive.

Fraternal birth order. Another area of research that has received attention in recent years is fraternal birth order. Researchers have studied whether there is a relationship between sexual orientation and the number of older brothers a male has. It is based on something referred to as the "maternal immune hypothesis,"[8] with the idea being that some mothers produce extra antibodies to a substance that is produced by male fetuses. The male fetus is essentially foreign tissue, so it is normal for the mother's body to produce some antibodies. But some mothers may produce more, and perhaps the more male children the mother has, the more antibodies. The thought is that there is then an increased likelihood that the brain will develop in a way that is more typical of females, which could translate into a homosexual orientation later in life. Some have claimed as much as a 33 percent increase in likelihood of developing this feminized pattern with each male child born.

Some recent studies have supported this hypothesis. Other studies have not.[9] Some who have expressed concern that this line of research may be embraced prematurely have also pointed out that the samples used may be biased in favor of showing support for the hypothesis. It is also important to note that even if the hypothesis were to be supported, it has been estimated that it would account for only about 15 percent of homosexual men. This estimation provides support for the idea of multiple homosexualities. In other words, many of the studies being conducted do not really address the "typical" homosexual or gay person; rather, they are studies of particular pathways to homosexuality that are quite limited and not likely to be the experience of most homosexual or gay persons.

A number of researchers continue to study fraternal birth order, and especially its relationship with handedness in predicting homosexuality.[10] Since handedness is something largely predetermined, it is believed that this correlation points to a prenatal development of homosexuality. Many studies have suggested that having older brothers increases the chance of homosexuality in right-handed males. They have also found that men who have no brothers have a higher chance of being gay if they are non-right-handed,[11] but these findings are not always as clear as is often supposed.[12]

What can be said about fraternal birth order, handedness, and sexuality? There are interesting findings out there, but the more work that is being done, the more complex it appears. There are also many ways people explain the different findings. So no one theory is really running away with a convincing explanation for now.

Animal models. Animal models of sexual behavior are also a common way to argue in favor of the biological hypothesis. This usually takes the form of showing that if an aspect of the animal's biology can be manipulated to increase same-sex behavior, then biology is the likely cause of homosexuality.

The study[13] of so-called "gay sheep" is one such example. There is an area of a ram's brain that converts testosterone to a compound that influences sexual behavior. In a rather sizeable percentage of rams (between 8 to 10 percent), there appears to be less of an ability to convert testosterone, leaving some to show a preference for other males.

Similar arguments from animal models have been made with flies that were genetically manipulated. Genetically manipulated flies, it turns out, can engage in same-sex behavior.[14]

The more basic criticism is whether animal models are good models for human sexual behavior. For example, we know that the courtship behavior of fruit flies is quite scripted and fixed, and I think most people would see a tremendous gap between the fixed courting behavior of fruit flies and human sexual behavior. Or at least I hope they would.

Genetic studies. These studies have also received a lot of attention. Several years ago a researcher published a study[15] that suggested there may be a region of the sex chromosome that is more likely to be shared by homosexual brothers whose family tree had homosexuality on the mother's side of the family. (This is another good example of the idea that we may have multiple homosexualities, since even if this study found what it was looking for, it would apply only to a very small percentage of people with a homosexual orientation.) In any case, the researchers reported a higher correlation than would be expected for this specific region of the sex chromosome. This same research team was able to conduct a similar study and replicate the findings from the first study. However, another research team was unable to replicate these findings.

So it remains open for further discussion. What can be said is that none of these researchers found a "gay gene." Remember how unique this group being studied was: they were male homosexual brothers who had homosexuality on their mother's side of the family tree. So there is no reason to think that, even if these findings are confirmed by another research team, it will explain a very large number of cases of homosexuality.

As I indicated above, there is no way to cover all of the studies that have been conducted to advance the biological hypothesis. There have been many, and new areas of research are sure to follow.[16] But they appear to share a number of weaknesses, which, if we look at each study carefully, we can begin to see. What is difficult is that few people take the time to look at the details, and most of us are probably just stunned by the sheer volume of studies that have been produced in the past twenty years or so. If they do not on their own merit provide a tremendous amount of support for the biological hypothesis, they sure do seem impressive when we merely look at the number of studies being produced!

So there are many studies, but these studies each have some important weaknesses. Why, then, shouldn't churches just dismiss these studies? I think the church should always be interested in truth wherever they can find it. We should reject the *misuse* of these findings, if people are pointing to them to say that the church has to change its teaching or doctrine about a biblical view of sex. But it is certainly possible that biology contributes in some way to same-sex attractions or a homosexual orientation. These studies may not provide direct support for what form that contribution takes, but it is possible, and I'd like to see the church be open to accurate findings from well-designed studies. The church has nothing to fear from science when science is done well.

My reading of the research is that it isn't a question of whether biology plays a role; the question is *how* does biology play a role? If it isn't like eye color or hair color, what impact might biology have? Biology plays an important role in so much of human experience, so it would be strange to act as though homosexuality was the one area that biology played no role whatsoever.

I appreciate Neil Whitehead's[17] attempt to explain this. He did so by looking at twin data for a number of traits, syndromes, and experiences, including homosexuality. Remember how I said that twin studies are interesting because they can tell us something about potential contributions from genetics and upbringing? Where does the contribution of genetics on homosexuality compare to things like alcoholism or Alzheimer's disease? How would it compare to the likelihood of hypertension? Well, the research to date places homosexuality below all of these other traits and experiences.

Whitehead says that same-sex attraction, most cancers, stroke, and criminal behavior are "all dominated by chance circumstances in life or individualistic reactions to them." So for Whitehead, the best answer to what causes homosexuality is that it is "mostly chance." To say that differently, same-sex attraction "is a highly individualistic response to what comes naturally in genetics and society. . . ."[18] As I have been suggesting, these various factors could range from childhood experiences to environmental events and how a person experiences and responds to them. As a colleague of mine says, perhaps this places different people on different pathways that can be amplified over time.[19]

How else might a person's pathway become amplified? It's hard to say. But let's look at the other experiences that are often discussed as possible causes of homosexuality.

Childhood Experiences

Psychoanalytic theory. The general idea behind the psychoanalytic theory of homosexuality implicates early parent-child relationships. For males, this includes being raised by an absent, distant, or critical father and an over-involved or "close-binding" mother. The experience is such that the male does not feel secure in himself as a male.

The young boy, consciously or unconsciously, patterns his personality after that of his father; this includes his father's pattern of being attracted to women. According to this theory, a young boy "identifies" with a beloved father and is encouraged and supported in that identification by a loving mother. A father who is physically or emotionally unavailable presents a challenge to male identification.

But the mother is important too. If the mother is threatened, she can undermine male identification, which "poisons" the father-son relationship (through criticism of the father or of men in general, for instance) or by working to make her relationship with the boy so powerful that separation from her is impossible. What is the result, according to this theory? A young man with a compromised sense of his own secure "maleness" and the resulting erotic attraction toward maleness in others.[20]

Few psychoanalytic psychotherapists publish studies to support this theory today. To be fair, there are few academic journals that would publish studies like this anymore. Most counselors who subscribe to this theory look for support from older studies conducted in the 1960s. One of the most influential studies[21] of over one hundred male homosexuals and one hundred male heterosexuals described the family dynamics we have been discussing. Fathers of male homosexuals were reported to be more detached, distant, or rejecting in relation to their sons. Also consistent with psychoanalytic theory, the mothers of the male homosexuals were reported as having enmeshed relationships with their sons.

The results of the study were based on the recollection of psychoanalysts of their patients' early childhood. The concern critics have raised is that there is no way to confirm that these dynamics were really in play. They are based on what the analysts said the patients told them, and some would say analysts working with male homosexuals might be more likely to remember such dynamics given the dominant theories about male homosexuality at the time. Also, since only patients were involved in the study, it is possible that these dynamics reflect those male homosexuals who are seeking help; how do we know if they represent all homosexuals or even all male homosexuals?

Another, smaller study[22] was published a few years later. It was meant to address some of these concerns. For example, the data was based on the self-report (rather than analyst report) of male homosexuals. Also, it included male homosexuals who had not been in therapy or analysis. What was interesting was that fewer than one-third of the male homosexuals reported the parent-child dynamics claimed by the earlier study. Also, over ten percent of the male heterosexuals reported the dynamics that were said to cause homosexuality.

A number of recently published studies have looked at family patterns that might predict homosexuality, given the psychodynamic understanding of homosexuality. For example, one study[23] followed children who had been physically or sexually abused or neglected. Childhood physical abuse and neglect were not associated with homosexual relationships as adults.

Another recent study[24] reported no significant differences between homosexuals and heterosexuals in how they remembered their relationships with their fathers. Indeed, the homosexual men in the study reported "warmer" (rather than "colder" or "distant") relationships with their fathers (and mothers) than did the heterosexual men.

I mentioned earlier that few psychoanalytic clinicians publish studies today on homosexuality. In this tradition, it is much more common to write up cases of specific people who have been seen in analysis. Therefore no large-scale studies appear, and it is unlikely that they will, which makes it challenging to either confirm or disconfirm the psychoanalytic theory of homosexuality. Despite that, the theory remains popular among many who provide services to change sexual orientation, including those in some Christian ministry circles.

To summarize what we know about psychodynamic understandings of homosexuality, the present data does not appear to provide much support for the view that poor parent-child relationships cause homosexuality as such. They may factor in among many other considerations, so we want to be aware of the range of potential influences while avoiding blaming parents or making them feel that they are the cause of homosexuality. My experience is that parents hear plenty of that message and may feel tremendous guilt if their son or daughter experiences same-sex attraction or announces a gay identity.

Childhood sexual experiences. Another popular theory in Christian circles in particular is that homosexuality is caused by childhood sexual abuse. Again, this can quickly run the risk of the sin of nothing-but-ism (i.e., "Homosexuality is caused by nothing but sexual abuse"). The research does suggest that people who have a history of childhood sexual abuse are more likely to say they have a homosexual orientation than those who do not report childhood sexual abuse.

In one large national study,[25] those who said they had a history of childhood sexual abuse were three times more likely to report a homosexual orientation than those who did not report childhood sexual abuse. An extensive review of the literature[26] conducted a few years later reported an even greater likelihood to identify as homosexual those among male adolescents who said they had been sexually abused by men.

A study I was involved in reported that homosexuals seeking to change their orientation had reported higher than expected rates of childhood sexual abuse.[27] The people we studied were seeking to change their sexual orientation from homosexual to heterosexual through involvement in a Christian ministry.

In the case of this particular study, it should be noted that these were all people seeking help. Since they wanted help, it is likely that they were more distressed than the average person in the general population. (That said, we found that they were less distressed than the average person who is in professional counseling.[28]) Since it is possible that one of the reasons they were seeking help was because they were sexually abused, we want to at least be cautious not to think that all or even most gay or homosexual people would have a history of sexual abuse.

A recent thirty-year longitudinal study[29] followed individuals who, as children, were sexually abused, physically abused, or neglected, and compared them with individuals who, as children, were not abused or neglected. As I mentioned above, neither childhood physical abuse nor neglect were associated with homosexual behavior or relationships. However, there was a connection between childhood sexual abuse and later homosexual experiences in adulthood. The men who had been victims of childhood sexual abuse were more likely to report homosexual experiences, although they did not tend to report cohabitation with the same sex or the ongoing relationships that might be more characteristic of a homosexual orientation or gay identity. It is possible that childhood sexual abuse complicated their sexual identity and led to some experimentation, but not to a fundamental sense of orientation or identity. Interestingly, in this study the relationship between childhood sexual abuse and adult homosexual experiences was present for men but not for women.

When we consider these studies, we need to always keep in mind that most victims of childhood sexual abuse do not identify themselves as having a homosexual orientation. Also, most people who report a homosexual orientation or a gay identity do not also report a history of childhood sexual abuse. So while sexual abuse could certainly complicate a person's understanding of their sexual identity ("Does the fact that I, a male, was abused by another male mean that I am gay?"), we shouldn't fall into the trap of treating it as a nothing-but-ism or thinking that it affects everyone in the same way.

Environmental Influences

What are some potential environmental influences on sexual orientation? In this section, I want to discuss the effects of additional family dynamics and society as a whole.

One of the controversial topics in our culture today is that of same-sex parenting. For years we have heard from experts that there is no difference between same-sex parents and heterosexual parents. However, recently researchers[30] analyzed over twenty studies that compared children raised by same-sex parents to those raised by heterosexual parents, and the results of their report called into question attempts by previous researchers to downplay differences. It is hard to say if these differences were downplayed intentionally or not, perhaps for political reasons. Regardless, the study that was published challenged the idea that "differences indicated deficits." In other words, the researchers made the argument that same-sex parents didn't need to be like heterosexual parents in order to justify their existence.

In a sense, the researchers saw such a position as a failure of nerve, a failure to say no to the idea that same-sex parents had to prove that they were not less successful or less worthy than heterosexual parents. What they argued was that even if there are differences between homosexual and heterosexual parents, there are no differences *that are of social concern.*

What does this mean? The researchers wrote: "Children with [homosexual] parents appear less traditionally gender-typed and more likely to be open to homoerotic relationships." Girls raised in these homes tended to wear clothing and play games that were "outside of cultural norms" (more tomboyish, I would assume), while boys raised in these homes also stepped out of traditional scripts for masculinity and were more nurturing. Young-adult children raised in these homes were more likely than those who were raised by heterosexual parents to engage in homosexual behavior. There were other similarities between children raised in these different types of homes, like the quality of parent-child relationships, but it is this last conclusion—that being raised by same-sex parents would increase the likelihood of engaging in same-sex behavior—that is a moral concern for Christians.

The researchers were offering a stronger argument in favor of same-sex parenting than we have typically seen. That is, they were saying that if as a culture we are okay with homosexuality among adults, we should not have any problem with increasing that likelihood among children once they are grown. (The authors of the review thought of these homosexual activities as simply "exploration," anyway.)

The reason I am including this information in the section on environmental influences is because the homes children are raised in play an important role in influencing them in many ways. So how might they influence homosexuality? I don't think it happens directly in an unavoidable, step-by-step fashion. Instead, the homes children grow up in, their experiences, and how they respond to these experiences can all be influential factors. Again, the impact will be different for different children. Being raised by same-sex parents appears to influence some children to at least explore or practice same-sex behavior, whereas they might not have under other circumstances.

Most children raised by same-sex parents are heterosexual, and most adult homosexuals were not raised by same-sex parents; so, again, we want to resist the tendency to make declarations about general causes of homosexuality.

Others have expanded far beyond family arrangements and child rearing to look at broader cultural or societal considerations. In one impressive study of homosexuality across cultures, a researcher who believes that homosexuality is more the result of social influences than biology or other factors, concluded:

> Where social definitions of appropriate and inappropriate behavior are clear and consistent, with positive sanctions for conformity and negative ones for nonconformity, virtually everyone will conform irrespective of genetic inheritance . . .[31]

It is interesting to compare how often homosexuality is reported in our culture, as well as how the amount changes in different places in the United States. For example, overall about 2 to 3 percent of adults report having a homosexual orientation. People are often amazed when I share these percentages. They say that it seems like a much higher percentage than that, given the amount of attention the topic receives today.

You might be interested to know that these percentages go up when we look at urban areas.[32] So the perception that more than 2 to 3 percent of the U.S. population reports a homosexual orientation is probably based on this higher percentage (closer to 10 percent) in cities, not to mention all of the coverage in politics, the media, entertainment, and other expressions of popular culture.

After his review of the different percentages in different settings across the country, theologian Robert Gagnon concluded: "In the United States today, the odds of a given child becoming homosexual increase dramatically depending on the social environment."[33]

Similarly, reflecting on some of the data related to environment, sociologist Edward Laumann made the following observation:

> Large cities may provide a congenial environment for the development and expression of same-gender interest. This is not the same as saying that homosexuality is a personal, deliberate or conscious choice. But an environment that provides increased opportunities for and fewer negative sanctions against same-gender sexuality may both allow and even elicit expression of same-gender interest and sexual behavior.[34]

Adult Experiences

As we think about the effect of adult experiences on homosexuality, I want to focus primarily on the decisions adults make about their behavior and identity. To some extent, this is different from the factors we previously talked about, because with biology, childhood experiences, and environmental influences, we were talking about what made someone more likely to have same-sex attractions and therefore become gay. But when it comes to the influence of adult experiences on becoming gay, we're talking about something that happens further down the line. Those same-sex attractions are usually already in place, so then the question is whether or not to embrace a gay identity and the sexual behaviors that express that identity.

A few years ago I provided a consultation to a young adult and his parents. He was grateful to hear that I did not think he chose his attraction to the same sex. He was worried that a Christian counselor might have thought his attractions were up to him. But when I shared with him the three-tier distinction between same-sex attraction, a homosexual orientation, and a gay identity, he was frustrated to hear that he still had choices to make—choices about behavior and identity. For him, he believed that once the question of what causes homosexuality was settled—once we were all in agreement that he did not choose his same-sex attraction—we would move on to helping his parents deal with it better. He thought they needed to be more supportive of his personal desire to advocate for gay rights and interests in the church and in the local community. He had not thought of himself as a person who still had choices to make. He hadn't thought much about whether he should engage in same-sex behavior or form his identity around his attraction. He assumed that was a foregone conclusion.

People often form a gay identity around their experiences of same-sex attraction by engaging in same-sex behavior and then declaring to themselves and others, "I am gay." They define themselves by this part of what they experience.

Let's return to Rick. Remember that Rick's mother asked if homosexuality was a choice or not. At the time I answered, "I don't think he chose to experience same-sex attraction, no. But I think we should consider what choices a person in his shoes has."

In other words, what is there to choose in this whole area of sexuality? Again, I don't think people choose to experience same-sex attraction. Yes, there are instances of radical feminists rejecting heterosexuality as a political statement, and there are also instances of people expanding their sexual repertoire to include same-sex behavior,[35] but that isn't what has happened for most people who seek a consultation around sexual identity.

Most people like Rick who experience same-sex attraction simply find themselves experiencing attraction to the same sex. But there are important choices to make, choices about sexual behavior and choices that will facilitate and reinforce a gay identity.

CONCLUSION

A person's attractions or orientation is not something they choose. They find themselves being attracted to the same sex. This is an important point for parents and the church to recognize. But people do have choices to make—choices about both their behavior and their identity. They can choose whether or not they engage in same-sex behavior, and they can choose whether they integrate their attraction to the same sex into a gay identity.

As for causes, what can we conclude? The American Psychological Association recently summarized the current understanding of the etiology of homosexuality when they stated:

> There is no consensus among scientists about the exact reasons that an individual develops a heterosexual, bisexual, gay, or lesbian orientation. Although much research has examined the possible genetic, hormonal, developmental, social, and cultural influences on sexual orientation, no findings emerged that permit scientists to conclude that sexual orientation is determined by any particular factor or factors. Many think that nature and nurture both play complex roles; most people experience little or no sense of choice about their sexual orientation.[36]

Do you remember Chris, the young person on the stage I asked you to picture in your mind earlier? When he looks to the church, I think it is okay for the church to acknowledge that the findings so far are complex, and that we don't know for sure what causes homosexuality. We can imagine that a host of factors probably contribute, and that those contributions likely vary in significance from person to person. We may want to offer him more than that, but we certainly don't want to be viewed as combative around the nature vs nurture debate, as though being right about nurture (rather than nature) is as important to us as he is.

Rick's parents also have questions to think about. What would it mean to them if they knew it was not a choice for Rick to experience same-sex attraction, but that he simply found himself attracted to the same sex? How would that influence how they view him and how they'd be as a resource to him? We will explore these questions in chapters 5 and 6, but they are tied to the topic of what causes homosexuality, and many families struggle with how to answer that and what it means for how they relate to one another.

The statement "We don't know what causes homosexuality" sounds like a reasonable conclusion. Maybe my original Web site idea was correct. But there is so much material to review and understand in order to reach that conclusion, and I hope you have a much better sense of that now.

Perhaps we could begin with some humility as we consider the topic of homosexuality. For the time being, perhaps it's okay to be an *etiology* (causes) *agnostic* (don't know). This may influence how we see and interact with the people we know and love who experience or contend with same-sex attraction, and guide us as we move forward.

TAKE-HOME POINTS

- People do not choose to experience same-sex attraction; it is something they find themselves experiencing.

- There does not appear to be any one cause of same-sex attraction or a homosexual orientation.

- There appear to be many factors that may contribute to same-sex attraction or a homosexual orientation, and these factors are probably weighted differently for different people.

CHAPTER FOUR

Can Someone Change Sexual Orientation?

I remember the day I went out to the waiting room to call Shawn back for his counseling appointment. He was in his mid-thirties, and when I called his name and invited him into my office, he looked up and took a quick glance around the waiting room. He seemed anxious. Maybe he just wasn't sure what to expect.

When he sat down he shared that he wanted help with his sexual attractions. He told me he'd had homosexual attractions since adolescence, and although he hadn't acted on them, his attractions were "pretty strong" and persistent. Shawn said he had been to a ministry to help him receive "healing" from his homosexuality, taking part in a thirty-week curriculum that lasted all fall and spring. After he completed it, he wondered what it meant that he still struggled with same-sex attractions.

He brought his concern to the ministry leader, who empathized with him, provided him encouragement, and invited him to participate in the same curriculum the next fall. Shawn went through the curriculum a second time. He said he benefitted from it; he learned new things about himself and his sexuality. He began to delve into his relationship with his father in particular, with the idea being that the shortcomings there may have contributed to his homosexuality. But at the end of the second thirty weeks, he found that he continued to experience same-sex attractions.

Again, he brought his experiences back to the ministry leader who said he could enroll in the program again the next fall. Shawn agreed. It was at the end of this third time through the same curriculum that he decided to talk to a counselor about his ongoing struggles with same-sex attraction. It wasn't that he didn't appreciate the ministry or the curriculum, or that he wasn't gaining insight into his behavior and attractions, but he was concerned that the attractions persisted after all this time. "Maybe," he shared with me, "I just haven't gotten at the core issue. Maybe I haven't resolved what's *really* going on."

Shawn's story is not as unique as it sounds. Many people experience homosexual attractions and put a lot of time and energy into finding an effective treatment, or they spend a lot of time in prayer asking God to provide them with healing. Many people I've met with in counseling or in a consultation have at one time asked God to take away their same-sex attractions.

While the idea of having ongoing struggles with homosexuality is not unique to Shawn, the decision to go through the same curriculum three times may be unique. Many people simply walk away if they don't receive the help they expect; others might look for professional counseling if ministry offers them limited success. This chapter will talk about whether or not homosexual people can change. Can anyone become heterosexual if they just try hard enough? And if not, are there other ways a person can "change" that we may want to consider?

Perhaps we should start by taking a brief look at some of the research. Interestingly, the American Psychological Association recently published a background document from a task force that reviewed many of these studies. They concluded that there was "insufficient evidence" to support claims of changes in sexual orientation.[1]

EARLY STUDIES OF CHANGE

Most of the earliest studies of change of sexual orientation were published in the 1960s and 1970s, prior to the removal of homosexuality from the *Diagnostic and Statistical Manual of Mental Disorders*. The *DSM* is the primary reference book used to classify various psychological problems or diseases. In 1973, the manual removed homosexuality from its list of illnesses, thereby declaring that it was no longer something that needed to be "healed."

When psychologists look at studies that occurred before the 1970s, what stands out is that they rely heavily on either therapist (or analyst) reports of change, or on clients' own sense of change.

I'm a counselor. Ask me how people do under my care, and I am likely to present a favorable image of my counseling. It may be true; but if it weren't true, how would someone know? That's the risk that comes with asking counselors or therapists how people did under their care.

So it is better to ask the client than to ask the counselor. But if you look at these early studies, the second thing you note is that the researchers relied on the client's own subjective measurement of change rather than more objective criteria. How did the person know there was change? How much change? Can others confirm this change or this degree of change? Of course, you could ask both the counselor and the client, but the weaknesses in asking both the client and the counselor are still present.

The other thing to notice is that few studies used a control group. A control group is a group of people who have the same concern (in this case, they would like to experience a change in their sexual attractions or orientation), but the control group receives no counseling during the same period of time. This helps researchers determine if the changes that are reported are a result of the counseling itself, or if the changes would have occurred regardless of whether counseling occurred.

Also, when you look at these studies from the 1960s and 1970s, you notice that none of them were long-term. People who were attempting change were not followed over time. They may have been measured at the start of treatment and again at the end of treatment, but few studies followed people for another year or more to see if the gains made at the end of treatment were sustained in the long run.

Another concern raised with these early studies is that what counted as "change" varied considerably from study to study. When asking if sexual orientation changed, it would be ideal if everyone measured sexual orientation the same way. But what we see in these early studies is that "success" included:

- Being able to engage in heterosexual sex
- A decrease in the amount of homosexual behavior
- An increase in heterosexual attraction
- A decrease in homosexual attraction
- Heterosexual marriage

That's a lot of different ways to define success and change!

To be fair, these studies were conducted the way most other studies were carried out in the 1960s and 1970s, so we have to be careful when we criticize them for not being conducted according to today's standards. No one in the 1960s was researching the way we do now in terms of how rigorous psychologists are in the way they design and carry out their studies.

But the older studies did have one thing in common: they all reported successful outcomes. Whether it resulted in behavioral change, self-reported change of attractions, or one's sense of sexual orientation, many people seemed to benefit from participating in therapy. By our calculations, about one-third reported (or were said to have experienced) "success" because of their involvement in therapy that was designed to change their sexual orientation.

In 1973, when homosexuality was removed from the *DSM*, there was immediately less interest among professionals in therapy to change sexual orientation. Interestingly, it was also during this time that we witnessed the emergence of faith-based ministries for homosexuality.

The American Psychological Association's (APA) current position is that there is "insufficient evidence" to support the claim that sexual orientation can be changed through involvement in change therapies or religious ministries. The benefits that can be gained through such ministries or through supportive counseling—benefits such as building social support, learning helpful coping skills, and so on—can be gained without focusing on change of sexual orientation. Although the APA's position is not the final word on the topic, it is good for us to keep it in mind.

MORE RECENT STUDIES

After a gap of several years, some professionals have become interested again in whether people can change their sexual orientation, and several studies have been conducted. Here are a few of the important ones, along with brief summaries of their findings.

MacIntosh Study. This survey,[2] conducted in 1994, included 274 psychoanalysts who were asked questions about their work with homosexuals. The psychoanalysts reported working with 1,215 homosexual patients, with reported change of sexual orientation for 22.7 percent of patients (23.9 percent of males; 20.2 percent of females).

Of course, as we talked about above, studies that rely on analysts to describe the gains made in treatment are susceptible to overreporting treatment success and underreporting treatment failure. However, this study and others really began to raise the question that hadn't been raised for a while: Can sexual orientation change?

The NARTH Study. The National Association for Research and Treatment of Homosexuality (NARTH) published a study in 1997 on change. It was a study of 855 persons who indicated that they had changed their sexual orientation or were in the process of doing so.

Among the findings, 37 percent reported being *exclusively homosexual* before the change process, 31 percent reported being *almost exclusively homosexual,* and 22 percent reported being *more homosexual than heterosexual* before the change process.[3] Nine percent ranged down through the rest of the scale.

After the change attempt, 15 percent reported being *exclusively heterosexual,* 18 percent reported themselves to be *almost exclusively heterosexual,* 20 percent reported being *more heterosexual than homosexual,* 11 percent reported *equally homosexual and heterosexual,* 23 percent reported being *more homosexual than heterosexual,* 8 percent reported being *almost entirely homosexual,* and 5 percent reported being *exclusively homosexual.*

It should be noted that this is an impressive number of people who had been or are currently involved in the change attempt. The study itself relied on the person's memory to indicate what their sexual orientation was before they attempted to change it. This method has its weaknesses. Ideally, you would ask the person to indicate their sexual orientation before the change attempt begins so that you have a "baseline" to measure from. In other words, you should measure sexual orientation at the beginning of a change attempt and then track that person over time to see if a change actually occurred.

Schaeffer Studies. Kim Schaeffer conducted a set of studies on people who tried to change their sexual orientation. The people involved in the study were found at an Exodus International ministry conference. Exodus International is an umbrella organization of Christian ministries for people who do not like the fact that they have a homosexual orientation. Some[4] of the participants completed questionnaires about their change attempt one year later.

The one-year follow-up found that 29 percent of 140 people reported a change in what Schaeffer called "feeling-based sexual orientation," which means a person's own sense of their change. Of the others, most (65 percent) were still attempting to change their sexual orientation, while 4.3 percent were unsure of whether to continue to try to change their sexual orientation, and 1.4 percent were no longer attempting to change their sexual orientation.

Spitzer Study. This was a study conducted by Robert Spitzer of Columbia University. Spitzer was best known for helping to get homosexuality removed from an earlier version of the diagnostic manual of psychiatry in the 1970s. He seemed like the last person who would conduct a study of whether sexual orientation can change. However, he apparently felt an interest in doing so after meeting several people who said that they had changed their sexual orientation.

Spitzer's study was published in 2003. He interviewed two hundred people who claimed to have changed their sexual orientation. Specifically, the people he interviewed claimed to have shifted from a predominantly or exclusively homosexual orientation to a predominantly or exclusively heterosexual orientation through some form of therapy.

Spitzer documented shifts in the way participants reported their own sexual orientation. This included changes in sexual attraction, arousal, fantasy, and yearning. Generally speaking, females[5] tended to show more significant shifts than did males, a finding that seems consistent with other studies of sexual fluidity among women who experience same-sex attraction. Before the change attempt, only about 2 percent of men and none of the women met Spitzer's criteria for *good heterosexual functioning* (which included frequency of heterosexual sex, satisfaction with heterosexual sex, and emotional satisfaction with spouse); after the change attempt, 66 percent of men and 44 percent of women met the criteria for good heterosexual functioning.[6]

Jones and Yarhouse Study. This three-year study,[7] which I conducted with Stanton Jones, was originally published in 2007. The study was originally of ninety-eight persons attempting to change sexual orientation through involvement in an Exodus ministry. Participants in the study were assessed initially and then between ten months and two years later, and then again about eighteen months later.[8] We gathered information from several of the best standardized questionnaires of sexual orientation, and also measured emotional distress.

When asked to share their identity rating (for example, homosexual, heterosexual, bisexual, other), 45 percent reported *positive change* over the course of the three-year study. This sometimes meant going from homosexual, bisexual, or other all the way to heterosexual, while at other times it meant a change from homosexual to bisexual or other. Forty percent reported no change, meaning they rated their identity label (homosexual, heterosexual, bisexual) the same at the end of the study as they did at the beginning. Eight people reported *negative change* and three reported *uncertain change*, for example, from bisexual to "other."

When we looked at the different measures of sexual orientation, we reported a significant or average decrease in same-sex attraction, the amount of which was likely meaningful. We also reported a significant increase in attraction to the opposite sex that was not as strong as the decrease in attraction to the same sex.

Participants were also categorized based on the information they shared about their change efforts. Fifteen percent fell into the category of *Success: Conversion* (to heterosexuality); 23 percent landed in the category of *Success: Chastity* (or the "freedom to live chaste," which was helped by a reduction in same-sex attraction); and 2 percent of the participants were categorized as *Continuing change effort*, which meant there was some reduction in attraction but not enough to describe themselves as having experienced success. In addition, 15 percent of participants were designated as having *No Response* to change effort; 4 percent as *Failure: Confused*; and 8 percent as *Failure: Gay Identity*. The designations of "failure" were only with reference to the goals of the participants themselves, in terms of being a part of Exodus to experience a change in attractions or orientation.

In 2009,[9] we presented additional findings, as we had been following participants for another three assessments that spanned a total of six to seven years. The results were presented at the American Psychological Association's annual conference. The average gains made early on in a person's change attempt appeared to be sustained over time. Again, there were more average gains away from homosexuality (diminished same-sex attraction) than toward heterosexuality (increased opposite-sex attraction). We asked participants which category best described their experience in Exodus, and *Success: Conversion* (to heterosexuality) rose to 23 percent of the remaining sample, while *Success: Chastity* also increased to 30 percent of the remaining sample.[10]

These are important findings for those who are considering whether to participate in a similar change effort. However, it is important to understand that usually we are not talking about 180-degree changes from gay to straight. Instead, the studies show a movement along a continuum of attraction, with the majority of the success coming from a decrease in same-sex attraction, which makes chastity not so much of a burden. These changes may also reflect an important shift in not only sexual attraction but also sexual identity, or a person's sense of themselves and whether or not they identify themselves as gay. Clearly, many people in the study did not view themselves as gay but rather began to form an identity around other aspects of themselves as persons.

What can we conclude about attempts to change sexual orientation? Let me start by saying that I think the two sides of this debate— organizations like the APA and other mental health groups on one side and conservative Christians and their organizations on the other— often speak past one another on this point. For example, I think those who argue that there is "insufficient evidence" of sexual orientation change are often thinking of categorical and complete change, as though sexual orientation were a light switch that is in one of two positions: on or off. Homosexual or heterosexual. Gay or straight.

On the other hand, Christians can sometimes add to the problem by claiming this kind of complete change happens frequently.

So is change possible? As I review the studies in this area, some people do report a change in attractions over time. For those who report a change, it tends to come in the form of a reduction in homosexual attractions, but these reductions are typically not complete. A smaller number of people also report an increase in heterosexual attraction. In some instances this may be attraction to the opposite sex in general; in other cases it may reflect attraction to only one individual of the opposite sex, such as a person's spouse. I think it may be helpful to everyone involved to recognize that 180-degree change or categorical change is less likely. That doesn't mean people shouldn't attempt change or feel discouraged about it, but it does help us identify the more likely outcomes. In some ways understanding this will free a person up to focus on other important considerations, such as vocation, stewardship, and Christlikeness. I will talk more about that soon, but before I do I want to discuss the often-made claim that attempting to change your orientation is harmful.

IS IT HARMFUL TO TRY TO CHANGE?

It had never occurred to Shawn that attempting to change might be harmful. The reason it came up in our discussion was because when someone requests help in the area of sexual identity, I ask them to sign an Advanced Informed Consent form. This document summarizes what we know and don't know about causes of same-sex attraction, various ways to respond to these concerns (professional counseling approaches and ministry approaches), the potential benefits and risks of counseling, and so on. It's this last point that was interesting to Shawn. As I'd mentioned, he'd never thought about the possible risks before.

I recommended that counselors who attempt to change sexual orientation provide an informed consent document so that patients would know what they could expect from their work in this area. Failing to provide informed consent has received a lot of criticism, since many people who are opposed to change therapies feel that potential clients are not given correct information on what they can expect.

I let clients know about these potential risks even though the counseling I provide does not focus on change of orientation counseling (or "reorientation" counseling). So what, then, does my counseling focus on? If you recall from chapter 2, there's a difference between same-sex attraction, sexual orientation, and sexual identity. My focus is on identity rather than on sexual orientation. One reason is because I believe such categorical shifts are rare.

Instead, I work on what most people can manage and experience change in: I look at how identity develops over time and how it can reflect a person's beliefs and values. I want to help people live their lives and identify themselves in ways that are in keeping with their Christian beliefs and values.

I shared these distinctions with Shawn because my sense was he still wanted to see his homosexual attractions diminish, and he wanted to experience a significant increase in his attractions to the opposite sex. We discussed the financial and emotional investment in counseling; it could be a mentally and monetarily expensive proposition, so it was important that Shawn think it over.

But perhaps the greater investment is the emotional one. We talked about the expectations people often bring to their counseling. The higher the expectations that he, for example, would soon have no more experiences of same-sex attraction, the greater the potential disappointment. This can be accompanied by feelings of guilt (for not feeling that he's tried hard enough or had enough faith), shame (for feeling that there is something wrong with him), anger, and so on. I talked to Shawn about how this disappointment could be directed inwardly toward himself or outwardly toward his counselor, God, or the church. This was especially important for Shawn to understand because we were not going to be attempting change of orientation but rather focusing on broader identity issues.

So, alongside the question of whether sexual orientation can change is the question of whether it is harmful to even make the attempt. Those who are opposed to people attempting to change their sexual orientation express concern about potential harm,[11] whereas those in favor of change attempts see this as a matter of informed consent for the person requesting such services. In any case, let's look at a few studies on this topic to give us some insight.

Shidlo and Schroeder Study. This was a study designed to prove that change of orientation therapies are harmful. They initially recruited people with just that intention, calling their research project "Homophobic Therapies: Documenting the Damage" (which was later changed to "Conversion Therapies: Do They Work?" apparently in response to people who were reporting benefits from participating in change therapy). In spite of the new title, the focus was really on whether it is harmful to attempt change. Most[12] of their participants did not succeed in changing their sexual orientation, and many reported experiencing harm as a result of treatment.

Shidlo and Schroeder also found that a modest percentage[13] of their participants reported benefiting from the change attempt, though not necessarily through experiencing a desired change of orientation.[14]

Schaeffer Studies. Those who were highly successful in attempting change of behavior and maintaining celibacy reported positive mental health on a variety of measures of happiness, loneliness, self-acceptance, and depression.

In another study by the same team comparing "ex-gays" to gay persons, "ex-gays" reported positive mental health, but those who identified themselves as gay reported even greater happiness and self-acceptance, and less loneliness.[15] So both groups were actually doing well, with the one group scoring higher on the various measures.

Spitzer Study. In the Spitzer study mentioned previously, the participants were more depressed[16] when they began their change of orientation attempt than they were[17] after their change of orientation attempt.

Jones and Yarhouse Study. In this study participants were given a measure of symptom distress that they completed at the start of the project and several times over the course of the study. On average, there was no evidence that involvement in this change process caused an increase in symptom distress or symptom severity. At the six- to seven-year follow-up, the only average change in symptom distress was toward slight psychological improvement.

Participants also completed measures of spiritual well-being. There was no evidence that involvement in this change process caused a decline in religious or spiritual well-being. In fact, every reported average difference indicated an improvement over six to seven years.

It is interesting, though, to look at how people answered the open-ended question, "How helpful has the ministry been so far?" Here are some of their replies that we reported in our book:

- " . . . made my walk with Christ closer . . ."
- "It was very helpful to increase my relationship with God, making it closer."
- " . . . get my hands on materials that are helpful to read."
- "I need that intermediate place between church and the rest of the world to be able to be honest . . . to have somewhere to be real."
- "They've helped me to find myself."

When asked about areas that reflect real change, participants shared several different thoughts. Here are a few of their comments:

- "I'd say what it's doing is reminding me of God's intimate care and reminding me of His care for me—that He's gentle and He will walk with me. I guess that's basically saying that it's okay to struggle."

- "I haven't acted out sexually in any way since I've been going. . . . It's gotten under the surface, helped me see the reasons why I did the things I did."

- "I think that God used it to let me know that I could struggle and still be accepted."

That is to say, most of the comments were not about a dramatic change in sexual orientation. Rather, participants tended to emphasize their relationship with God, their experience of God's love and acceptance, and spiritual growth. That's not to say that change did not occur, but it is striking to see that when an open-ended question allows people to talk about "real change" and what was particularly helpful to them, they tend to gravitate toward spiritual themes and messages of acceptance.

CONCLUSION

To summarize what we have covered so far, it appears that most people will not change their orientation, if by that we mean moving from "completely gay" to "completely straight." But change can occur along a continuum. Sometimes same-sex attraction does diminish, and in one of the most recent studies of attempted change through Christian programs, many participants who continued in their change effort reported a decrease in attraction to the same sex so that chastity was not the burden it had been before. A smaller number of participants also reported an increase in attraction to the opposite sex or to their spouse. Change of orientation is rarely complete or categorical, and many of those who report change may still experience some attraction to the same sex at times. It does not appear to be intrinsically harmful to try to change, especially if a person has realistic expectations.

Sometime later I met with Shawn again. He shared with me that he was beginning to sit with the idea that his attractions were not going to change. He shared that this was hard for him to admit to himself, and he wondered if he had done enough, if he had tried hard enough. He wondered out loud if it was sinful to come to terms with his homosexuality. Let me be clear that he did not endorse homosexual relationships. He was not concluding that he should embrace a gay identity, which in his mind was synonymous with approving same-sex behavior. Rather, Shawn was struggling with whether, as a believer, he could stop struggling to actively change his sexual orientation. He wondered if he was letting God down or doing spiritual damage to himself.

We talked about his worries. He shared that his understanding of Christianity and homosexuality was that he had an obligation to change his orientation. If he wasn't experiencing change, it meant there was something wrong with him—he wasn't trying hard enough or he didn't have enough faith in God's ability to heal him. It would take a lot for Shawn to figure out how he was going to respond to the pressure he felt to keep attempting change of orientation.

What does it mean for a person to come to terms with his or her same-sex attractions? We will discuss this more in chapter 8, because we want to look at how the church tends to respond to chronic or besetting conditions. We will also need to come to a better understanding of what makes it difficult to see homosexuality as a more enduring experience for most people who are attracted to the same sex.

TAKE-HOME POINTS

- Although some people do experience a change in sexual orientation, most experience modest gains, and many share that they continue to have same-sex attractions at times.

- It does not appear to be intrinsically harmful to try to change sexual orientation, especially if a person has realistic expectations.

- Where people may struggle the most is with unrealistic expectations or messages that they are not trying hard enough or do not have enough faith.

PART TWO

HONEST ANSWERS TO QUESTIONS FACING FAMILIES

What If My Child or Teen Announces a Gay Identity?

I picked up the phone at work and found myself talking to a very anxious mother. She had a son, age five, who she was worried was gay. I asked her to back up a moment and give me a little more information. She shared that he was doing "girlish things" that worried her. She said he was too focused on her and not interested enough in "being a boy" or "doing what boys do" or wanting to be more like her husband.

I asked, "What do you mean by 'too focused on you'?" She went on to share how her son, Jeremy, was much more into her and her things: "He has been going through my purse, and he wears it around the house; or he puts on my shoes and tries to walk in the heels. He'll get a hold of my makeup, like lipstick, and put it on."

She went on to share that this had been going on for the past year. "It was funny at first," she shared. "It was cute. My husband and I would laugh, and so would my parents. I mean, it was kind of funny to see him prance around with my purse or whatever. But it seems like he is more about me than he is about my husband. It's like he's *identifying* more with me than with my husband. I don't know; maybe it's nothing. But tell me . . . is Jeremy gay?"

This chapter addresses two different questions. The first is, How do we know if a child is likely to experience same-sex attraction? That is what Jeremy's mother was asking. The other question is, How should parents respond to a teen who is identifying as gay? We will address that as well.

IS MY CHILD GAY?

The first question is fueled by parents being worried about the future. All parents envision what their own lives will be like, as well as the lives of their children. When their children's experiences don't seem to be unfolding in a way that matches their own expectations, they get anxious.

Few parents want their children to struggle with homosexuality. Even with the increased social acceptance and trends in the media and entertainment industries, most parents have a sense that homosexuality would be a difficult path. Those difficulties might have to do with the social rejection their child would feel, but they could also have to do with the losses parents themselves might have to deal with. For instance, it saddens many parents to realize that their child won't date the opposite sex, marry, have biological children, and so on.

Add to this the Christian parents' concerns about a struggle against a pattern of behavior that is seen as sinful, and the anxiety mounts.

And it's not just anxiety. Often there is shame as well. It is almost a cultural shame, or evangelical subcultural shame, that can come with being a part of the evangelical Christian community. Shame is an emotion someone experiences when they feel that something in them is fundamentally flawed. Shame can be felt in a community when a person feels that there is something wrong with them or their family—not with something they are doing but with some aspect of who they are. Parents in evangelical Christian circles often feel that there is something wrong with them because their child experiences same-sex attraction or announces a gay identity. We will talk more about this experience of shame, but it is important to see that the seeds of shame are often planted when a parent first fears that a son or daughter might be gay.

Not incidentally, I think this kind of subcultural family shame can lead parents to take extreme positions. One position is to suffer in silence. Rather than risk the shame of letting others know what's really going on, they prefer to struggle with this in isolation. It can be tremendously emotionally draining.

The other position a parent may take is to embrace their child's gay identity and become more of an assertive advocate, openly disagreeing with the traditional Christian sexual ethic out of a position of being protective of their child or teen.

So how do we know if a child is likely to experience same-sex attraction? You should note that in asking the question this way, I am trying to draw on some of the principles covered in chapter 2. I don't tend to talk about "gay youth" or "pre-homosexuality." I think it is premature to talk in those terms when we're dealing with children, and I also think such language lends itself to the "discovery" metaphor you were introduced to in chapter 2. I do not think this metaphor is particularly helpful to young people because it draws on assumptions that often go unstated (such as that this is who a person "really is"), and that beg the question.

A child's sense of themselves as either male or female usually develops by age two or three. The development of cross-gender interests can begin between two to four years of age, although parents who are concerned about such behavior do not tend to ask for help until their child is elementary-school-aged, which was essentially what happened with Jeremy.

It is clear that Jeremy demonstrates behavior that is more stereotypical of girls. That is actually one of the most consistent experiences shared by adults who have a homosexual orientation: gender nonconformity in childhood. What is gender nonconformity? It is engaging in the stereotypical play and interests of the opposite sex. For example, a boy might be more interested in playing with girls' toys, dressing up as a girl, playing house, and so on. A girl might be more interested in playing with action figures, playing cowboys and Indians, playing with trucks, and so on. There is a lot more latitude here for girls, as parents are not usually very concerned about tomboyish behavior. But for boys the "box" is pretty small as to what they can and cannot do. When boys do things outside of that box, parents get anxious.

Not conforming to gender stereotypes occurs within two major areas of concern: gender identity concerns, such as the rare condition referred to as Gender Identity Disorder (GID), and adult homosexuality.[1]

GID is rare, and children with this disorder will insist they are the opposite gender, showing extreme gender nonconforming behavior. For example, a biological female will insist she is or wants to be a boy. Such children also show stronger interest in stereotypical games, dress, and interests of the opposite sex.

What causes gender nonconformity? Those who emphasize nature (that is, biology) argue that such early gender nonconformity probably shows that biological forces are at work. Those who emphasize nurture (that is, the child's environment or experiences) argue that influential psychological forces have shaped the child from the day he or she was born. Both groups are in agreement that children who display gender nonconformity are more likely to grow up to become homosexuals. However, not all children who struggle with gender nonconformity have problems later with either gender identity or sexual identity.

What Can I Do About My Child's Gender and Sexual Identity?

Interestingly, GID does appear to respond to parental intervention. Recommendations include ignoring and gently but consistently redirecting extreme gender nonconformity, affirming the biological sex of the child, modeling appropriate gender behavior, and reinforcing it when the child expresses it themselves.[2] If a boy is showing a strong preference to play with his sister's Barbies, for example, the parent might ignore it (rather than criticizing him for his interests) and redirect his attention to other activities that the parent hopes to foster interest in.

While we know that gender nonconformity is a part of an adult homosexual person's history, it is less clear from research that intervening in childhood will prevent homosexuality. In other words, interventions that seem to aid in preventing gender identity issues do not appear to resolve sexual identity issues. Why can we appear to prevent gender identity concerns but not sexual identity concerns at this time? We don't know. But most GID kids grow up to report a homosexual or bisexual orientation.[3]

I don't want to suggest that preventing homosexuality absolutely can't be done, but prevention often comes back to the question of cause. As we discussed in chapter 2, we don't at this time know what causes homosexuality. If anything, we have multiple possible influencing factors, both from nature and nurture, that may contribute to same-sex attraction. These factors appear to vary from person to person, being "weighted" differently. Recall the principle of equifinality, which is the idea that there are many ways to one outcome. We also said that there are multiple homosexualities, recognizing differences among individuals and differences between men and women.

What we know and what we don't know affects prevention. For example, since we know that smoking causes lung disease, we know that to prevent lung disease it is important to stop smoking. Since we don't know what causes same-sex attraction, it makes it more difficult to know what to say to parents about prevention.

However, since we believe there is some indication of environmental factors (again, they are likely weighted differently for different people), some parents may decide to follow some guidelines, such as working hard on improving the child's relationship with the same-sex parent, creating a home with clear boundaries, preventing destructive messages about sexuality and sexual behavior, and fostering healthy relationships with peers.

Parents typically begin by taking a careful inventory of their family dynamics. They can look for ways to improve their relationships with their children so that they are encouraging and respectful, and so they reflect healthy boundaries in which the parents know where they end and where their child begins. These methods also provide an opportunity to help children identify specifically with their same-sex parent. This involves instilling a healthy experience of gender identity by affirming a son or daughter's gender so they have a clear idea of what it means to be a boy or a girl; and as parents, showing them healthy examples of being male or female.

Toward this end, parents can look at their own relationships with one another. Are they in a stable marriage that models a healthy way of relating to and being respectful of their spouse? From this perspective, parents affirm a young person's biological sex as male or female by seeing a male (father) and a female (mother) relate to one another in healthy and respectful ways.

Sex education is also an important part of this approach. One of the leading Christian resources is *How and When to Tell Your Kids About Sex* by Stan and Brenna Jones. Their approach is really about shaping character in your children over time. It is not about having "the talk" in the teen years, but rather focuses on being in an ongoing relationship with your children, one in which you take the lead in identifying and capitalizing on teachable moments, pointing out destructive messages, inoculating your children against those messages, and preparing them to have a firmer grasp on healthy sexuality and sexual expression.

For parents who follow this path in responding to their child, it is important to be encouraging of the behavior you want to reinforce rather than critical of the behavior that makes you anxious. It may be more effective to ignore (rather than criticize) the unwanted behavior, redirecting a child away from it and toward other behavior you want to foster. This will take time and patience. It will also help to model the behavior you are looking for, since, as mentioned above, the same-gender parent plays an important role in showing the child what it means to be male or female.

To sum up what we've learned, parents can encourage and gently but consistently redirect their child in order to foster a more secure gender identity. This will likely resolve gender identity confusion, but it is not as clear what impact it would have on sexual orientation. Since there is some indication of environmental factors in homosexuality, parents may decide it is important to them to follow some of the suggestions that have been helpful in resolving gender identity confusion. But even in cases in which it appears to resolve gender identity confusion, in my view it is also important at some point for parents to reflect on how they will respond if their older child were to experience same-sex attraction after puberty. Parents need to be prepared for different experiences and think about how they will demonstrate love and regard for their son or daughter.

Toward that end, parents may benefit from reflecting on what they are doing and why. For instance, they may want to take these steps regardless of whether or not they can expect to prevent homosexuality, simply because these steps reflect good parenting. The parents I have worked with have all wanted to demonstrate unconditional love toward their children regardless of what their children experience later in adolescence. I think that is a helpful and constructive way to think about these things.

We also need to consider the parents' fears and anxieties. With Jeremy and his mom and dad, their greatest concern at the time was whether Jeremy was gay. I discussed what we know and do not know about the causes of homosexuality, but I also discussed with them that the concern about "being gay" is a matter of identity. In some ways that rests in the hands of the older adolescent or adult who experiences same-sex attraction. Remember that experiencing same-sex attraction is not the same thing as having a gay identity or being gay.

Train Up a Child

One of the primary verses Christian parents struggle with is Proverbs 22:6. It reads, "Train a child in the way he should go, and when he is old he will not turn from it." When a teen child announces he or she has a gay identity, parents often struggle with whether they have trained their child improperly. Or, to bring us back to the question of prevention, if they had raised their child properly, would this issue of homosexuality ever have come up?

I think this questioning is a misapplication of the verse. We are called to raise our children properly, and that training extends to creating a home environment in which they hear about a relationship with Jesus and know who He is and about His love for them. It may also extend to some of the things we are discussing about clear affirmations of a young person's gender identity and self-worth as created in God's image. However, we do not know that this necessarily prevents any number of human experiences or conditions that reflect the fall.

It is important to make this distinction: It is one thing to raise a child to know God's law and to have a relationship with Christ; we equip them to make decisions by influencing their character in the way we raise them to regard God's Word. But it is another thing to make decisions for our older teens. They are going to be making adult decisions soon. Most young adults actually hold the values their parents hold in the most important areas of morality, even though they may differ significantly in things like music and clothing. But some do not mirror their parents' values, and there is a point at which parents need to recognize that the decisions their older teens make are their own decisions. Parents simply need to be there for their children if or when those decisions lead them down a path they'll later regret.

In the context of influencing a child's character, I think it can be important to help young people respond to their own impulses and bodily urges. This starts at a young age, and it is a critical part of education, as it shapes the character of children over time. Even if we don't know at this time what causes homosexuality, we at least want young people to know different ways to respond to the feelings they have. These responses will contrast sharply with current cultural messages about "self-actualization" and being "true to yourself," concepts that are far too thin to be Christian.

Jeremy Revisited

Let's return to Jeremy and his parents. I worked with them on decreasing their anxiety about Jeremy's behavior. I encouraged Jeremy's father to be more involved and to take specific steps to encourage his son: to affirm his son as a boy and to lay the groundwork for his son to identify himself with his father. I also encouraged Jeremy's mother to be intentional with Jeremy about his behavior. She could ignore and gently redirect Jeremy toward the kinds of interests she and her husband want to foster without overreacting to his behavior or being expressly critical of Jeremy.

I also worked with Jeremy's parents on what it would mean if their son were to experience same-sex attraction. They needed to face this possibility and, rather than fear it, find a way to affirm their son and express unconditional love to him. They needed to be in a position to be helpful resources rather than additional sources of pressure and anxiety as he grows up. Jeremy's parents appreciated the opportunity to sort out these issues. They were experiencing a lot of anxiety that was keeping them from responding in the way they wanted to. But after our work together, they felt they now had a plan, a way to interact with Jeremy that would address their concerns within a realistic framework. This meant preparing their own hearts to express love and support to their son as he grows up and moves toward sexual maturity.

We turn our attention now to the other major question addressed in this chapter. The first question dealt with how parents can know if their child is gay; the second question deals with what to do about a teen who already says that he or she is attracted to the same sex.

WHAT IF MY TEEN ANNOUNCES A GAY IDENTITY?

A mother who met with me in my office told her son, Phil, to wait in the waiting room. She walked back with me, and when I closed the door, she said, "I'm at the end of my rope. I don't know what to say, and I don't know what to do. I'll be honest with you: I'm frustrated by this whole situation because I did not carry this boy in my body for nine months and then raise him for seventeen years to have him turn around and be a homosexual. That's not how we raised him, and that is unacceptable."

I asked her to have a seat. She shared that Phil's father was active in the military and unavailable for counseling at this time. She shared that they were both Christians, and they did not approve of same-sex behavior. Over the past several weeks she had come to find out about her son's experiences of same-sex attraction through a friend of hers whose daughter was Phil's age. The teens were both on a popular online social network, and there were some suggestive pictures of Phil "posing" and "messing around" with other guys. The mother was embarrassed to see these, and she was angry about it. She confronted Phil, and he said, "Yes, I'm gay...or bi. I'm not really committed to any one label."

Phil's experience mirrors that of many young people who experience same-sex attraction. By the time Phil's parents knew about it, he had already talked to numerous friends who provided him with ample support for his gay identity.

Describe Rather Than Declare

In our culture today, "coming out" (short for "coming out of the closet") means telling another person that you are gay. Coming out is synonymous with informing someone else of your gay identity. But there is another way to approach this. What I have found more helpful is to think of coming out in terms of sharing with others the fact that you experience same-sex attraction.

Talking to others about your experiences of same-sex attraction essentially uses the three-tier distinction (discussed in chapter 2) between same-sex attraction, a homosexual orientation, and a gay identity. It focuses more on the *descriptive* aspect of attraction when it comes to informing others about your experience. This seems to be particularly helpful with teens who are confused or have questions about their identity. The emphasis is then placed on being able to share with their parents that they experience same-sex attraction and that they want to bring their parents into greater awareness of what is happening in their lives.

Contrast this with the teen who says to his parents, "I'm gay." To parents this often comes across as not merely a description of what's going on but instead as a pronouncement or declaration. And often it can be, precisely because teens frequently figure this out alone or with their peers and only later share the results (their identity) with their parents. This can happen for a lot of reasons, but remember that teens are often quite invisible, particularly in the church, so they may be wrestling with their own sexual identity in isolation. They may feel unable to share with their parents or others for fear of judgment or expressed disappointment. But this fear that leads to shame and further isolation can give way to a pendulum swing to the far side if a young person concludes that this is "who they are." It can lead to an identity declaration that seems rather extreme to the unsuspecting parent.

When it comes to family relationships, declarations can lead to emotionally charged exchanges among family members who quickly become entrenched in their positions. This is one reason I encourage young people to describe their experiences ("I experience same-sex attractions") rather than form an identity around their attractions. This can help them avoid polarized "positions" with their parents and move them toward a more honest and respectful relationship.

When I talk to parents, I encourage them to be descriptive too, or to at least keep descriptive language in mind. I don't want them to insist that their teen think of it in a descriptive way; that's up to their teen. But as parents, they can choose how they think about their son or daughter, even if their teen is making a strong declaration. Is your son saying, "I am gay and wanted you to know who I really am"? Or is he saying, "I experience same-sex attractions and am sorting out what that means"? There is a significant difference. But even if a teen is making a strong declaration, it may be more helpful for parents to respond as if their teen were talking about attractions, and to then be open to learning about the path they have been on and where they are today. What often lies beneath that declaration is fear that they will not be accepted or loved. The stronger the declaration, often the better prepared a person is for rejection. Unfortunately, the stronger declaration can also sometimes lead to a greater risk of being cut off from parents.

What makes this difficult, as we learned from Phil's mother, is that a parent's emotional reaction to the disclosure alone can be overwhelming. Many parents experience disbelief, sadness, guilt, and sometimes anger, as was the case with Phil's mother. But anger is what we might think of as an "umbrella" emotion. Underneath that umbrella are a lot of other feelings, often "softer" feelings of confusion or sadness. These are much more helpful to discuss than anger.

So I ask parents to take the lead in not negatively reacting to declarations. Keep in mind a few key things. First, remember where your son or daughter is developmentally. Adolescence is a time of trying on different identity roles in order to settle on something that feels right to them. They may play a different role at home than they do at school or at work or with their peer group or with their youth group, and so on. This is normal, although it obviously becomes more complicated when sexual identity questions are in the mix.

Second, keep in mind that teens in our culture receive cues for making sense of their sexuality primarily from our culture. The primary script they read from around same-sex sexuality is the gay script (see chapter 2). This script is compelling. And, frankly, the church has not put much effort into providing an alternative script. Worse, we have not really prepared young people to think about how their faith is real and vibrant and impacts all aspects of their lives, including their sexuality and sexual behavior. This also includes what it would mean to find meaning and purpose in other aspects of who they are besides just expressing themselves sexually. Keeping this in mind can enhance your sense of empathy for your teen and offset the tendency toward anger or rejection.

A third thing to keep in mind is that your teen may have been dealing with his or her homosexuality or gay identity for a long time, and they are only now bringing you into the loop. Therefore, they are in a different place than you are when it comes to thinking about these issues. Most parents learn about their teen's homosexuality long after their teen's peer group knows, as teens tend to disclose their attractions to friends first, then maybe a sibling or in some cases a youth pastor. After that, mothers are typically told, with fathers often being the last to know.

Keeping the Long View in Mind

It may be helpful to recall some of the events that are part of a teen forming a gay identity. As we mentioned in chapter 2, when we ask young adults who are gay[4] what they experienced growing up, they tell us that they were first aware of same-sex attraction as young as age eight or nine. They say they engaged in same-sex behavior around age thirteen or fourteen, and then labeled themselves as gay a few years later, around age sixteen or seventeen. First same-sex relationships were not typically reported until age nineteen or so.

On the other hand, some of these events are different when we look at Christian college students who experience same-sex attraction. For example, the age they were first aware of attraction to the same sex was closer to twelve or thirteen. Most found these feelings confusing and did not engage in same-sex behavior. This may be one of the reasons so few preferred to label themselves as gay. Although about one-third of the Christians we surveyed initially thought of themselves as gay (at about age seventeen), only a small percentage (14 percent) took on the label "gay" for themselves or were ever in a same-sex relationship (20 percent).[5]

I have a few observations based on these studies. It is interesting that sexual behavior comes before labeling. Maybe behavior helps confirm or consolidate an identity that a person already suspects or is questioning. This may be one more good reason to delay sexual behavior, a message that parents can give to all teens regardless of whether they experience same-sex attraction.

Also, initially thinking of oneself as gay is not as common for Christians in our study, and it did not always translate into a gay identity label that was sustained over time. In another study, we reported that it took many more years for Christian young adults to sort out their sexual identity questions than it did for non-Christians, with these issues often extending into their mid-twenties and even into their early thirties.

This suggests to me that parents would do well to hold back from reacting emotionally to their teen when they find out about same-sex attraction. You want to express care and concern but not strong emotions that might evoke a defensive posture.

Also, it is helpful to take a longer view than what is happening *right now*; be available to your teen as they are sorting out sexual identity issues, recognizing that where they are today may not be where they are a year from now or five years from now or ten years from now. Your relationship with them is important and can be sustained throughout these times of questioning and labeling, and you will want to build on the foundation you've already laid so you can be available to them as a resource in the months and years to come.

What About the Needs of the Parents?

I mentioned earlier that parents often struggle with whether they did something to cause their teen to experience same-sex attraction; and this understanding of causation is particularly common in Christian circles. Christians often look at parent-child relationships or childhood sexual abuse rather than other possible explanations, which is in part because Christians feel compelled to reject the biological hypothesis for homosexuality. As we discussed in chapter 3, we really don't know what causes homosexuality, so in counseling sessions I try to be sure to communicate this to parents. They could expend energy focusing on things they may have done wrong, but none of us has any idea whether those things caused their teen's homosexuality. Their energy would be better spent in developing the relationship they want to have with their teen from now on. The question to ask is, How can I be a resource to my teen over the next year? or What is my adolescent going to need from me moving forward?

In suggesting this focus, I don't want to gloss over the grief or sadness that many parents feel. And as I mentioned earlier, if they have been angry they will soon find out that their anger is really an umbrella emotion, and underneath that anger are feelings like heartache or loss. Those feelings are important to at least acknowledge. Parents will need to come to terms with what their teen's sexual identity questions may mean for their family. There may be a sense that dreams have been lost, such as not having grandchildren through traditional means. But even while acknowledging their grief, parents must keep in mind that the situation might change; this is not necessarily the last word on their teen's sexual identity. This is a tricky balance to achieve.

Meanwhile, during this time parents often feel isolated. You may think that you can't speak with family members, friends, or others you usually count on for support out of a fear of stigma or embarrassment. This can be particularly true in conservative Christian circles. It is important that you identify safe, trusted people with whom you can share your thoughts and feelings. Do not try to go through this alone.

It is also important that parents attend to their marriage and turn toward one other rather than away from one other. Most parents have mixed feelings of love and disappointment, concern and guilt, and so on. Often one parent emphasizes a certain emotion, such as anger, which can lead to the other parent focusing on another emotion, such as concern. A conflict can ensue between parents who actually share many of the same feelings but to different degrees. Parents benefit from talking to one another and keeping communication open as they sort out the range of feelings they have at this time.

For children who are in their mid- or later teen years, parents should focus on being supportive and identifying trustworthy resources while also recognizing that challenging questions may arise regarding behavior and relationships. For example, at this point and even later (in a child's adult years), families may need to negotiate rules or standards with regard to same-sex relationships. This might include time away from home with friends, dating relationships, access to various social networks, and so on.

Some parents feel stuck trying to sort out how to love their son or daughter while not saying or doing things that might condone same-sex relationships. This takes tremendous emotional energy and complicates relationships that may have previously been viewed as "low maintenance." This change may increase a parent's sense of loss. During this time it is okay to ask for the space you need as parents to make decisions. There is sometimes a lot of pressure on parents to respond in ways that may go against their beliefs and values. It may be helpful to take time to think through your beliefs and find ways to communicate them in the context of love and regard for your son or daughter.

I mentioned earlier in the chapter that it is important to be aware of the influence of cultural shame on the family, particularly in the evangelical Christian subculture. This sense of shame within one's community can lead parents to struggle in isolation from others. On the other hand, it can have a reverse effect; that is, it can lead parents to fundamentally change how they view homosexuality so that they end up endorsing it, behavior and all, for the sake of the relationship with their teen. This can also lead to conflicts within the evangelical community, and some families end up leaving those communities to find support from others.

These are difficult issues for families to navigate in order to come to a place of mutual understanding. It may be helpful to seek out a trained counselor to guide you as your family tackles these challenges.

Phil Revisited

When I first met Phil and his mother, Phil had been depressed for four weeks, and his mother had never seen him like this. I asked more about what had happened since the time she discovered the pictures and confronted Phil. She said she contacted a Christian ministry that encouraged her to cut Phil off from his friends who supported his gay identity. She had done that almost immediately after she discovered the pictures and began looking for help. She was responding out of her strong feelings of fear and anger. Phil was upset about this, as he had been close to some of these friends for a few years, and he grew increasingly depressed. When she asked for a few minutes to talk privately with me, she admitted she was worried that he might hurt himself.

I worked with Phil's mother on the issue of safety and depression first. I asked her to reconsider the friends. Generally speaking, while I can appreciate the advice she said she was given, it is never a good idea to remove social support if there are not other sources of support readily available.

Phil was able to have contact with these friends again. Yes, they supported his gay identity, and this was difficult for Phil's mother. But Phil was also able to come out of his depression and was soon no longer at risk of hurting himself.

Phil said he respected his parents' religious beliefs, but he did not consider himself to be a Christian. We focused then on being respectful of his parents' beliefs and values while he lived under their roof. This was a practical discussion of life in their home together. He was open to this, and he realized that it wasn't fair for him to act entitled; both he and his parents were in two different places on this, and they would have to find a way to respect each other as he neared young adulthood.

I spoke to Phil about the three-tier distinction between attractions, orientation, and identity. I discussed with him the importance of what same-sex attractions mean to him. He heard from me that some young people consider same-sex attractions to be the central part of who they are; the attractions are given great weight in determining their sexual identity, and they conclude their search for identity with the declaration, "I am gay." Other young people attribute their attractions as a part of their experience but are not the defining aspect of themselves as a person. They form their identity around the fact that they are male or female, or they form their identity around their faith tradition, which happens when someone says that their primary identity is "in Christ."

He was open to this other perspective, but after he had some time to think about it (several months), he shared with me that he'd decided his primary identity was gay. He preferred the modern sociocultural identity label over more descriptive accounts. This was difficult for his mother, but she was glad that he heard other options and was at least willing to listen to and consider other ways he might think about himself. Family counseling, then, became a place to discuss these decisions and to find ways to improve communication within the family, particularly as Phil turned eighteen and was moving out of the home.

It wasn't that Phil was choosing to experience same-sex attraction, but he did have choices to make now—choices about his behavior and identity. His parents had choices to make too. They could change their beliefs and values about same-sex behavior and identity, they could cut their son off, or they could consider ways to be in a relationship with their son while retaining their beliefs and values. They chose the latter. The use of descriptive language was helpful to these parents, as they found ways to be with their son and respect his decisions even though they did not approve of his behavior.

Counselors rarely have "perfect endings" in therapy. After all, from Phil's perspective his parents did not come around to his "side." They did not support his current identity as gay, nor did they change their beliefs and values to support same-sex behavior. From his parents' perspective, Phil did not come around to their "side." He did not accept the offer to participate in counseling to explore other options to a gay identity. He heard about the three-tier distinction and the potential value in using more descriptive language, but he did not choose to take this opportunity to explore a range of options. I also worked with Phil's parents to take the long view; that even though Phil gave thoughtful consideration to describing his experiences rather than forming a gay identity, it does not mean the decisions he made today will reflect the decisions he will make in the months or years to come. I'll share more about this in the next chapter.

On a positive note, this family did learn to relate to one another as a family. They made room for considerable differences of opinion, and by staying in a relationship, they retained the ability to have an impact on one another over time.

In our last meeting, Phil thanked me for working with him and his mother. Phil's mother also thanked me for working with her and with Phil. She appreciated having a relationship with him and finding ways to draw on the love she has for him even while she is opposed to some of his decisions in this important area.

TAKE-HOME POINTS

- There is no one cause of homosexuality, including your relationship with your child.

- Gender nonconformity is probably the most consistent experience adults with a homosexual orientation report from their childhood.

- If your teen discloses same-sex attraction, stay calm and listen, keeping in mind the obstacles that get in the way of listening.

- Remember that your teen was aware of his or her same-sex attractions long before you knew about it. Give yourself time to process.

- Avoid polarizing as a couple.

- Use descriptive language to discuss feelings of attraction.

- Take the long view—decisions made today may not reflect future decisions.

CHAPTER SIX

My Adult Child Announced a Gay Identity: What Now?

Mr. and Mrs. Sanchez sat down in my office. Neither knew how to begin. The silence began to enfold us, which often means we are about to discuss a very difficult topic, something quite painful. Eventually Mr. Sanchez said they called because their daughter, now twenty-three, recently announced to them that she was a lesbian. Mr. Sanchez began to tear up. Mrs. Sanchez continued, "She just said it like it was a matter of fact—like it was something that we'd understand. It was like we stepped into a discussion she was having—but we had no idea. I mean, *no idea*. You have to understand that although she didn't date a *lot* in high school or college—she was quite involved in competitive sports—she dated *some* boys and certainly could talk about them and had showed an interest. She went to dances. She went to prom. She may not have been as *into* boys as some of the other girls, but she certainly dated. I was dumbfounded. I was shocked, to say the least. I'm still shocked; I don't know what to say."

Mr. Sanchez found some words. "Some people talk about women's sports as places where this is fairly common, as a place where there may be many lesbians. If we had known that at the time, I don't think we would have supported it as much as we did. And now she's with someone—a young woman we've known through our daughter for years. She's been to our house many, many times. Well . . . now they are apparently a couple."

"It's like she's been dishonest with us by being in this relationship all this time," said Mrs. Sanchez. "How could she be in this relationship, know what we believe as Christians, and then pretend they were just friends all this time? Did she think it wouldn't bother us?" she asked no one in particular.

After several seconds of silence, Mrs. Sanchez continued, "So is it true about female sports?"

"We definitely would like to hear your thoughts about that," said Mr. Sanchez. "But we are also wondering what to do now. She wants to come home to visit, and she'd like for both of them to come— our daughter and her 'friend,' and I just don't think either of us is comfortable with having them stay with us. My wife and I are in just such a different place than our daughter, and we're frankly surprised that she doesn't 'get it.' "

WHAT NOW?

In this chapter we address the questions that arise when an adult child announces a gay identity. We're building from where we left off in chapter 5, which focused on whether homosexuality can be prevented in childhood and how to respond to a teen who announces a gay identity. There are some unique challenges that come up in adulthood, however, and we want to think through these together.

In my experience, young adults who talk to their parents about being gay are much more likely to make a declaration than request assistance. Many teens are not asking for assistance either, but more of them have questions than the young adults I know. This may be the result of a number of things, including simply the length of time they've been experiencing same-sex attraction and sorting it out on their own or with a close circle of friends.

I encourage parents of adult gay children to keep in mind the distinction between attraction, orientation, and identity. As with older teens, it is sometimes helpful to think descriptively about a person's experience of attraction and possible orientation, as this reminds parents of what their adult child faces every day. This will give parents some clarity about what they are really concerned about: Their grief or loss may be focused on the challenges their child faces in same-sex attraction or orientation. The question of what a person does with their attraction is limited more to identity and behavior. If parents have objections to identity and behavior, that can be discussed after parents recognize that their adult child is not choosing to experience their attractions or orientation.

Related to this is the gay script. Keep in mind that the gay script is compelling to those who experience same-sex attraction, including your adult child. Remember that we as a Christian community have not offered an alternative script that your child would even be aware of. What they often believe about the church is that they would be rejected out of hand. But we as a community haven't really prepared them to think about their sexuality in any other way. I hope that this reminder will foster a sense of empathy and compassion in you as parents, even if your adult child is making choices with which you disagree.

Many of the young adults I've met with have brought their parents in for help, meaning that they want support for their parents rather than asking for help for themselves. When I meet with parents in these circumstances, I encourage them to set a tone of mutual respect by listening.

This is harder than it sounds, so let's not rush past it.

LEARNING TO LISTEN

It is hard for parents to listen when they hear their adult child talk about long-standing same-sex attractions, particularly if they weren't aware of them or if there had been a history of dating the opposite sex. Asking an adult son, "What about when you took Marsha to the prom?!" is less of a question than it is an accusation. The parent is in essence saying, "You were either lying to us then or you are lying to yourself now."

This is not listening. In fact, a comment like this is often expressed out of confusion and frustration rather than concern. If, as parents, what your son or daughter is saying doesn't make sense to you, invite him or her to share experiences and memories with you without interrupting with your own account of them. When he or she is done, you might tell them that you remember some of the events differently, which may be why you are finding it confusing. That is an honest response and more constructive than denying what your child is saying or insisting on a different account. The more you model good listening and extend that to your adult child, the more you can expect your child to extend the same courtesy to you. The alternative leads to both you and your child becoming entrenched in your positions.

It is hard for parents to listen when they are reviewing in their minds the decisions they made that, looking back, they feel may have contributed to homosexuality. It is very common for parents to wonder if they caused their adult child's experience of same-sex attraction. From the parent's perspective, this might include not being involved enough in their son or daughter's early childhood, strained parent-child relationships in adolescence, or allowing or encouraging certain activities, such as sports for girls or drama for boys. If this is something you as a parent are worried about, you are not alone. But the point here is that the more parents focus on this the less they are able to listen to their adult child. This may lead your adult child to conclude that you've already filled in the history, conveying to them that you don't feel the need to listen.

Unfortunately, parents have ample opportunity to read accounts in various Christian resources that implicate parent-child relationships. So when I encourage parents to look for education and support, they often come across the message that they are likely the cause of their child's homosexuality. I have not found this to be particularly helpful to them.

Remember what we know—and don't know—about the causes of homosexuality. This is one of the hardest things for parents to hear because it doesn't give them certainty. In fact, I think many parents are susceptible to the messages that they are to blame precisely because they at least get some kind of clear explanation of what went wrong, as well as something they can do to counter it. I disagree with this message. I think it is more accurate to say that we do not know what causes homosexuality, and that there are likely multiple causes that are weighted differently for different people.

In addition to the scary uncertainty, "not knowing" can also translate into the assumption that their child is making this choice. It is important for parents to remember that people do not choose to experience same-sex attractions or a homosexual orientation; they simply find themselves with these attractions. Initially these feelings are experienced during the early teen years for most people.

That being said, as we've talked about earlier, same-sex attracted people do have choices to make about their identity and their behavior. But these choices will be made against a backdrop of a powerful gay script that equates attractions with identity. This script is compelling, and it is understandable why your child is drawn to it as a way to make sense out of his or her attractions and sense of identity.

Let's return to the question of causes of homosexuality and how to respond. If there has not been a good and healthy parent-child relationship, family members can decide together to improve what has been difficult in the past. But to place the blame for same-sex attraction on the shoulders of the parents is not only a misreading of the complex findings on homosexuality, it also adds guilt to parents who are often all-too-ready to accept it. When parents focus too much on the cause and, in particular, their sense of guilt, they are unable to listen.

Keep in mind that I don't think we have particularly compelling reasons to believe that improving the parent-adult child relationship today will resolve the homosexuality for the adult child. Parents who wish to improve their relationship with their child should do so simply on the basis of it being the right thing to do rather than with the view that it will solve the riddle of homosexuality.

It is also hard for parents to listen when they do not see from their adult child the values that they thought they held in common. Conservative Christian parents sometimes share with me that they had assumed their child would make certain decisions about identity and behavior even if they did experience same-sex attraction. They thought they would choose chastity or celibacy in keeping with their Christian view of sexual morality. When their adult child suddenly starts talking about a same-sex relationship, it can be particularly difficult.

Often young adults hear the Christian message about sex in marriage as a message without hope for them. They may have already tried to change themselves or asked God to change them. Or on the other hand, they may not see it as an issue that God cares about. Meanwhile, they see the church saying no to what they experience as a meaningful relationship, and they hear the emphasis on heterosexual marriage as signaling a life without intimacy for them.

Listening isn't the only thing parents can do, but it is an important first step. Listening doesn't guarantee agreement or common ground on such a divisive issue, but it is a good place to begin because it validates your adult child's experiences and lets him know that you are not going to dismiss him or his views.

KNOW WHAT YOU BELIEVE

If asked, be prepared to explain your beliefs and values. I think it is always more helpful to talk positively about what you believe than speak negatively about what you oppose. Even if asked about homosexuality directly, I would encourage parents to step back into a discussion that provides a context for what you believe. This might mean talking about a Christian view of sex and marriage rather than a discussion of Leviticus 22:18.

If you are saying to yourself, "I've never had to actually say what I believe," you are not alone. Many parents have not been in this position, perhaps assuming it was a given or that they essentially assented to what their church has taught, much like they believe in the Trinity but do not necessarily have a well-thought-out argument to support Trinitarian doctrine. So you may not have given it a great deal of thought, but if this is something that could create a gap between you and your adult son or daughter, it is important to reflect on what you believe and why.

What if you are not asked to talk about your beliefs and values? Your adult child may assume that he or she already knows what your beliefs are, and therefore may not feel the need to ask. Or they may not want to hear your beliefs reiterated, not wanting to step into further conflict or disappointment. It can be difficult for children, even adult children, to hear disapproval from their parents.

Even if your child assumes they know what you believe or acts like they don't want to hear it, I think at some point it is important to communicate your beliefs to your adult son or daughter. But you gain the right to share your views by listening first. This is going to be increasingly important as our culture moves away from a consensus on homosexuality. Beliefs and values that were once held in common are not any longer.

You can share with your words, in a face-to-face discussion, but you may also find it helpful to write out what you believe. This could take the form of a letter you send to your adult child or it could be something you keep for yourself, using it as a reference point for when you have a conversation with them. Some parents find it helpful to have a third party present, perhaps a counselor, pastor, or family friend. The idea is that this person can help diffuse some of the strong emotions that can come up for either of the parents or the child.

I mentioned above that it is better to speak positively about what you believe than negatively about what you are against. It is also helpful to be transparent. In sharing what you believe, you may find it constructive to talk about choices you have made or wish you had made in response to God's call on your life. This might mean talking about how God has worked in you, providing direction and guidance in the decisions that have shaped you, helping you develop your own sense of spiritual maturity. After all, this is what you want for your adult child—a personal, vibrant relationship with God through Christ. Don't assume that they do not have a personal relationship with Christ, even in the context of choices they are making. We really don't know how the Holy Spirit is working in their lives at this moment. But you can share what God is doing in your life and how the choices you have made have been in response to God's leading.

Scripture and Related Spiritual Issues

Some parents want to review with their adult child what Scripture teaches about homosexuality. This is an extension of sharing one's beliefs and values, but it is a little more specific. This is more common in Christian families that see Scripture as an anchor point for how they view all of life and how they ought to live.

It is not that reviewing Scripture independently or together is a bad idea, but parents often approach this with the hope that a clear reading of the Bible will convince their adult child that the parents are right and the child is wrong. Many adult children, however, do their homework. They have often read or are at least familiar with recent attempts to interpret Scripture in a more gay-affirming way. I encourage parents to be familiar with this literature in order to come to an understanding of what their child has been reading, and to also get to know critiques of those views.[1]

Remember, however, that this is not just an intellectual exercise for your adult child. It is not a theological debate, as important as theology is in this case. In my experience, young adults who have been able to respond positively to the Scriptures and the Christian sexual ethic have felt genuinely convicted by the Holy Spirit. They are convinced that they should say no to what they experience as a natural desire and longing for connection in favor of saying yes to a personally fulfilling life in Christ. In order to empathize with your child, it is important you understand that this desire feels natural and it is a genuine longing for connection with another. Your child's sexual behavior feels to them like an expression of their sexuality, and as Christians we do believe that sexuality is important to what it means to be a person. So this leaves the same-sex-attracted adult with a genuine dilemma—saying no to one thing in order to say yes to something else that is less tangible. The personal fulfillment that comes with stewarding sexuality takes time to experience; it is more like a spiritual discipline, like silence or fasting. It can be tremendously rewarding, but not until a person is accustomed to it.

An additional spiritual issue we should consider has to do with resisting the urge to speak harsh words, using anger to correct and bring an adult child "back in line." James 1:19–20 reads, "Everyone should be quick to listen, slow to speak and slow to become angry, for man's anger does not bring about the righteous life that God desires." If parents want changes to come in their adult children, getting angry, saying harsh words, or rebuking them is probably not the best way to go about it. That is not how change occurs. Indeed, my experience is that anger will only further entrench a person in the position they have taken. There is an important role here for the Holy Spirit, softening a person's heart so that they can be open to other ways of experiencing their own lives and the decisions they are making.

Setting Limits

It is one thing to do your homework—to read up on a Christian sexual ethic and to sort out what you believe and why. It is another thing to discuss your beliefs and values with your adult child. But the most challenging thing of all is making decisions that reflect those values and affect your adult child. Parents vary considerably in whether or how they set limits.

For example, some parents focus primarily on their relationship with their adult child, not setting any limits around events such as holiday gatherings, birthday parties, and so on. Their child is welcome, as is his or her partner. The parents may not approve, but they do not set ground rules as a means of expressing that disapproval.

Other parents have little to no contact with their adult child. They may prefer this over the pain they feel when they see their child with their partner.

More often, however, parents set some limits based upon their beliefs and values. This will often be expressed through what they do and do not allow at family gatherings, holidays, and other events. Keep in mind that these events are symbolic, both for you as parents and for your adult child. For parents, limits are typically set around whether their adult child and his or her partner will stay with them, whether they will celebrate birthdays or holidays together, whether they will share a meal at the parents' house together, and so on. The Sanchezes, for example, may struggle with whether or not their adult daughter and partner can stay with them over Christmas and New Year's. They may decide that their daughter is welcome but that she cannot bring her partner. For the Sanchezes, this is done to avoid sending a message that they approve of the relationship. For their daughter, however, this may be interpreted as their not wanting to have a relationship with her, since she and her partner have a serious relationship, one in which such an invitation feels like an insult.

Another couple I know has been invited to their son's home, where he and his partner live, but they have not felt comfortable being with his son and his partner in their house. This couple has preferred to meet their son and his partner for a meal at a restaurant, which is a compromise they both can deal with at this time. They extend themselves as far as they can while reserving the right to uphold a boundary that is symbolic to them. For his part, their son has decided not to cut them off. He is not saying, "Come to our house, accept us as a couple in this way, or you will not continue to be able to see me." Both the parents and the adult child are trying hard, stretching themselves to some extent, to maintain contact in a difficult situation.

Still another mother I know has prayed about a similar situation with her adult son. She does not agree with his choices about same-sex behavior and relationships. She has met his partner, and she appreciates him and has gotten to know him and both of them as a couple. She would say that she does not experience this as a compromise. She believes her son knows she disagrees with his choices, and he has shared that understanding with me. But she wants to be as connected to him as she possibly can. He and his partner can come to her home, but her son has decided not to stay overnight out of sensitivity to his mother's values.

I tell parents that they are naturally inclined to see limit setting from their own point of view. Sharing a meal with someone in your home, for example, may mean you approve of their actions. You may not want to send the message that you endorse their relationship, and you see certain events as possibly communicating this. But try to see the limit-setting from your adult child's perspective.

Limit-setting is symbolic; it means something to everyone involved. That doesn't mean you shouldn't set limits based on what you think is right or feel you can handle, but it does mean that you are not the only person to consider. Your adult child is affected by what is decided. Good, clear communication is essential here, and even that may not guarantee that all conflicts will be resolved. Although there are no guarantees, adult children are more likely to accept your limits if they understand your reasoning, even if they disagree with you.

Take Care of Yourself and Your Marriage

Much like when a teen comes out, there is a tendency for parents to polarize when an adult child announces a gay identity. Remember that polarization happens when each parent almost becomes a caricature of a set of real and strong emotions that both parents likely feel. It is most common for this to take the form of anger from one parent and love from the other.

I am using anger and love to represent strong emotions that might feel more like disapproval or support. Anger is a socially acceptable way for parents, especially fathers, to respond to other feelings that may be harder to express. These other feelings include hurt, loss, grief, disappointment, and confusion. It can be helpful for the parent who is carrying these feelings to identify them and talk about the softer feelings underneath. This keeps them from being expressed only as anger and can prevent cutoffs.

The parent who expresses love for the family is often feeling protective of the adult child, frequently in response to the other parent who is expressing anger. This is how parents can become polarized. Try to use this image: In tennis, you can either play singles or doubles. If you play singles as a couple, you are on the opposite sides of the net, playing against one another. On the other hand, if you play doubles, you are playing together as a team. You want to be sure that how you talk to one another reflects a genuine desire to be on the same side of the net, as it were. It is most likely that each of you feels some anger (or confusion, grief, sadness) and love (protection). You want to give each other the space needed to express a range of emotions, and if this is difficult for you or if it feels like you are "locking horns" over what is happening with your adult child, you may find it helpful to discuss this with a third party, such as a counselor or pastor.

But taking care of your marriage involves more than just being on the same side of the net. It also means taking active steps to turn toward each other during this difficult time. I encourage couples to draw on resources like John Gottman's *Seven Principles for Making Marriage Work*,[2] where he talks about principles of satisfied couples, including the tendency to turn toward one another rather than away from one another. I encourage couples to apply these principles during this confusing time of potential conflict.

It is also important to take care of yourself. Remember that grief is a common response for many couples, and one or more partner may struggle with depression. Self-care involves having a framework or structure in place that is good for you. It includes diet and nutrition, regular exercise, social support, and spiritual disciplines, such as corporate worship, reading of Scripture, and prayer. If depression does not respond to these kinds of regular structures or framework, it may be helpful to meet with a counselor or other mental health professional.

Let me say a little more about social support. Having an adult child who identifies as gay is the kind of challenging situation that for some Christians is especially isolating. There may be family shame around admitting that an adult child experiences same-sex attraction or is making choices about identity and behavior. This can sometimes lead parents to one of two extreme responses: either uncritical acceptance that challenges community norms and the Christian sexual ethic, or isolation away from the much-needed social support that could help them during this difficult time.

I encourage couples to develop a social support structure that might include a pastor, a counselor, family members, and several close friends with whom they both feel comfortable sharing what is happening in their lives. Again, some families will be quite open and transparent about what is going on while others will function in isolation. They may focus instead on work or other demands on their time, but with little sense of purpose or quality of life, and too often with little sense of what it means to take care of themselves individually or as a couple.

WHERE IS GOD IN ALL OF THIS?

The strong emotions couples feel in response to their adult child's identity and/or behavior can also be reflected in their feelings toward God. Couples might feel anger or confusion in particular. Often they don't know if it is okay to express this anger, and if so, how to do it.

First, I do believe it is okay to express to God the feelings you have toward Him. He already knows that you feel this way—you are essentially just acknowledging it to Him and to yourself. Anger toward

God is often really confusion. Parents feel confused about what is going on and where God is in their circumstances. This is not unusual.

Just as you have a choice to turn toward your spouse or away from your spouse during this difficult time, you have a choice to turn toward God or away from Him. This is one of the most important decisions you face, and I encourage you to turn toward God—to be honest about what you feel and about your worries and concerns for your son or daughter, for the future, for the different family relationships, and so on.

Even expressing anger toward God is an act of turning toward Him. It has been said that the opposite of anger is not love; it is indifference. Being angry or confused is not the same as indifference toward God. He knows what you feel; He can handle your expressing it and sorting it out with Him.

I don't have an easy answer for where God is in all the pain that parents feel, but I have found certain readings to be helpful for parents during this time. Resources in facilitating this level of honesty in personal relationships with God include Jerry Sittser's *When God Doesn't Answer Your Prayer* and Philip Yancey's *Disappointment with God*.[3] These kinds of readings have something in common: they are not afraid to be transparent before God. There is an act of faith to be found in this kind of honesty. It is as if the believer has nowhere else to go, so they persist in the relationship with a determination that is found in desperation, drawing at times on their own history of God's faithfulness to them or, if they don't have that much history to draw upon, drawing on the history of God being faithful to His people throughout the Old Testament.

In the end, I don't think God abandons us in our confusion. I have seen God respond to the honest questions parents ask, but sometimes this means sitting in pain and letting God attend to us in time. I can't say this is necessarily why God allows these difficult circumstances, but I do believe God will be present with us, providing us with what we need and often surprising us with His grace and mercy.

HOW WILL IT END UP?

I have seen a number of different outcomes for families in which an adult child announces a gay identity. Although it's rare, sometimes the relationship ends altogether. It may be too difficult for the parents or not sufficiently supportive for the adult child, and they essentially agree to go different directions (or there was a cutoff by one side).

But most often parents and their adult children work out a relationship based upon mutual understanding and respect. Sometimes parents come to change their beliefs and values about homosexuality and sexual behavior; other times, they retain their values but focus primarily on the relationship they have with their child. They may disapprove of some of the decisions their adult child is making, but they know that their child knows this, and it does not have to be restated. Rather, they build bridges based on genuine love for the child—a love that is fueled by the same Christian faith that tells them about sexual behavior and sexual morality.

In some cases I have seen adult children make the decision to dis-identify with a gay identity after several years in a relationship. There are a number of testimonies in which individuals have said that they knew what they were doing was wrong. But they will often go on to say that the relationship was real and that the relationship met their emotional needs. Leaving their same-sex relationship is sometimes the most difficult step they've taken. In these cases, there is still so little support for them in the church it is a wonder they stay on this path. I can't say that this is a common outcome, but it does happen, and when it does, those who have made this decision tend to talk about it as a response to the work of the Holy Spirit in their lives.

It is difficult to know what may unfold in the years to come. I encourage parents to take a long view, to move past the immediate reaction they have today, and to think about the kind of relationship they want to have with their adult child, recognizing that where they are now may not be the last word on sexual identity and relationships. To take a long view means taking care of yourself and your marriage, keeping lines of communication open with your child, and being honest and transparent about your own life. It can be helpful to stay connected in order to be someone your child can come to. I don't think this outcome—the work of the Holy Spirit in a person's life—can be manipulated or orchestrated; rather, real relationships are characterized by empathy and support, as well as honesty and integrity.

CONCLUSION

When an adult child announces a gay identity, parents often struggle with many questions about how best to respond. There are many obstacles to listening, and overcoming these obstacles is an important place to begin. The more you are able to listen, the more you can come to a genuine understanding of your adult child's experiences. Listening also lays a foundation for future discussions in which you might share your understanding, beliefs, and values.

Before leading with your values, reflect on what it is you believe and why. This may be the first time you've done this in such an important area. Be familiar with the arguments on both sides of the theological debates about Scripture and the traditional Christian sexual ethic. Also, take care of yourself and your marriage, as well as your relationship with God. Take a long view of the present circumstances so that your immediate reactions are not the defining ones for how you relate over time.

TAKE-HOME POINTS

- If your adult child discloses a gay identity, stay calm and listen; give yourself time to process.
- Remember the three-tier distinction and use descriptive language to discuss feelings of attraction.
- Limit setting is symbolic, so try to see it through your eyes and the eyes of your adult child.

- Attend to your marriage by turning toward your partner rather than away.

- Turn toward God by sharing with Him how you feel, including strong negative feelings like anger or confusion.

- Take a long view of the circumstances.

CHAPTER SEVEN

What If My Spouse Announces a Gay Identity?

"It hit me like a ton of bricks," whispered Sherri, once she settled into the sofa. "In fact, a ton of bricks would have been an improvement on how I was feeling. I was stunned. You could have pushed me over, because I had no idea." Sherri was talking about the day she realized that the gay pornography she found on the home computer belonged to her husband, James. Sherri didn't open up emotionally about it, not at this time. She could bring herself to talk about it only if she kept it at an emotional arm's length.

Sherri was a forty-two-year-old woman who had been married to James for seventeen years. They had a daughter, fifteen, and a son, age thirteen. When Sherri's daughter stumbled across some of the pornography on the computer, Sherri investigated and found some of the files. She immediately thought it was their son's, which was certainly a concern. But when she brought it to James to talk about, she quickly realized that it was James who had been looking at the pornography—not their son.

He sat across from her and said, "I'm gay. I don't know what to say. I think it's been part of my life since as long as I can remember, but I've always tried to hide it; I've tried to deny it." Sherri doesn't remember a lot about what happened next. "I was stunned. It was the most surreal moment, I'll be honest with you. I was confused and couldn't really process what he was saying. One minute I was thinking about what this might mean for our son and how we could approach him as a team or whether James would talk to him about it; the next minute my world was upside down. Everything I knew just seemed to be wrong now. I didn't know what to think."

Many of the couples I have known come to see me because they are at a crisis point similar to what Sherri and James experienced. The spouse found homosexual pornography on the computer. Or maybe one of them discovered their partner was having a homosexual affair. These crisis points are not just about deception or unfaithfulness, but also about fundamental questions of identity—are you who I thought you were? What does this mean about me? What does this mean about our marriage? What does this mean for our future?

MIXED-ORIENTATION MARRIAGES

Mixed-orientation marriages are marriages in which one spouse is a sexual minority (he or she experiences same-sex attraction regardless of identity label) and the other partner is heterosexual. What do we know about mixed-orientation marriages?[1] Let's look, first, at why people say they enter into these marriages.

It turns out that people enter into these marriages for many of the same reasons heterosexual people enter into any marriage: they love their spouse. They care deeply about them and feel that marriage is the next logical step or expression of that love. Other frequently cited reasons include a desire for a companion or social expectations that they get married. Others want a spouse and children. Still others admit that they married as a way of working out sexual identity conflicts. (This last reason is sometimes the result of well-meaning friends or even pastors who have counseled in this direction. Having met with a number of these couples, I would say that marriage should not be seen as a way to work out sexual identity questions or conflicts.)

In most cases the spouse of a sexual minority does not know that this is even an issue. Like Sherri, they frequently have no idea that the person they married is sorting out these concerns. They learn about it through disclosure or discovery. Disclosure, as painful and challenging as it may be, is better than discovery. Disclosure means coming to one's spouse and honestly sharing experiences of same-sex attraction with the idea that as a couple you should make decisions about the next steps.

Let me share an example in which disclosure occurred well in advance of marriage. Jessica was a forty-five-year-old woman. She had strong Christian convictions and was secure in her personal faith. When she met with me she shared that she was in a mixed-orientation marriage with Frank for the past fifteen years. Jessica came to counseling because of conflicted feelings about how her local church was discussing the topic of homosexuality. She was personally a conservative on matters of sexuality, believing that God intended for sex to occur between a husband and wife in a monogamous marriage relationship, and that behaviors that fall outside of that relationship are not God's intention for sexual expression. At the same time, Jessica shared that she felt she had a lot in common with sexual minorities who identified as gay or lesbian. It pained her to hear a message that went against a Christian sexual ethic, but it also pained her to hear fellow believers denigrate sexual minorities. It made her feel less safe to be in the church; she didn't know what they would think of her if they knew about her lifelong struggle.

With respect to her marriage, Jessica shared that she disclosed her same-sex attractions to Frank prior to getting engaged, telling him about her past sexual encounters with women during college. Frank understood that Jessica continued to be attracted to women. These attractions were in the background most of the time, but certain relationships brought her attractions to the foreground.

She asked me for help in understanding her attractions and coping more effectively with them. A recent same-sex relationship had been particularly difficult for Jessica, as it drew her in and caused her to wonder if it really was an unhealthy emotional connection. Even though this same-sex emotional relationship came to an end, Jessica wanted to identify ways to respond more intentionally to her longings while prioritizing her marriage and family, as these relationships reflected her primary commitments and values.

In contrast to Sherri's experience of discovery (unexpectedly finding James' pornography), Jessica disclosed her attractions and past behavior to her husband before they were even engaged. She thought that she was in a different place with her attractions when they wed, and she was genuinely surprised and confused when her attractions to women seemed to resurface.

So Sherri learned about her husband's same-sex attractions through discovery, whereas Jessica disclosed her same-sex attractions to her husband before they were engaged. But whether the heterosexual spouse finds out through disclosure or discovery, mixed-orientation couples face some of the most difficult terrain imaginable, and there are few reliable guides to help couples walk through it. It often feels like there are no places to get a firm footing.

STAGES OF RELATIONSHIP CHANGE

Although the details of how to hike through this terrain are unique to every couple, the general landscape looks like this: *awareness, emotional response, acceptance of reality,* and *negotiating a future.*[2] The first stage, *awareness,* refers to the time of disclosure or discovery that we've been discussing so far in this chapter. Sometimes this takes the form of a humble, tearful sharing of something painful that the sexual minority spouse has struggled with for years. This might come after the discovery of an affair, with the sexual minority becoming apologetic and regretful of past behavior. On the other hand, the sexual minority could claim a gay identity and show no regret for his or her actions or deception. For Sherri, the stage of awareness was characterized by an event she will never forget: coming across gay porn she assumed was her son's. For Jessica, the stage of awareness came well before marriage but then seemed to reassert itself several years later. Frank was surprised to hear about it, but because of the past disclosure, he had a framework in place to understand what she was talking about. Frank was patient with the process of sorting out Jessica's confusion about her attractions, whereas Jessica was distraught and troubled by what the resurfacing of her feelings meant about her and about the future of their marriage.

Emotional response refers to what the spouse often experiences as a result of disclosure or discovery. Common emotions include confusion, shock, disbelief, or anger. This time in a person's life can last for weeks or months or even longer depending on the specific circumstances. Sherri was hit "like a ton of bricks" when she came across the gay porn, while Frank had an idea of what might be happening because of Jessica's previous disclosure.

Acceptance of reality refers to coming to terms with the fact that one's spouse is emotionally and sexually attracted to the opposite sex. The spouse who is working through all of this is also often trying to come to terms with any sexual behavior on the part of the sexual minority spouse that has been an expression of his or her same-sex attractions. This part of the process is similar to what happens when someone discovers that their spouse has had an affair.

Sherri was grateful that her husband's actions were limited to self-stimulation and images of gay pornography (and that her husband's actions did not extend into same-sex relationships that would put both of them at risk for STDs, etc.). But at the same time, it took her several months to really come to terms with his attraction to the same sex. She had many questions about where the attractions came from, how long he had felt such attractions, what it meant about her as a woman, and so on. These are normal questions, and it can be helpful to have a counselor present to confirm that they are normal and to create a safe place to discuss them.

Even though Jessica's attractions hadn't resurfaced for many years, at least Frank had a reference point for them. It wasn't as hard for him to accept the fact that she had same-sex attractions as it is for a spouse who is hearing about it for the very first time. But he did have to accept the reality that Jessica's attractions had not gone away.

Negotiating a future is the last stage, and it has to do with deciding as individuals and as a couple about the future of the marriage relationship. Sometimes this decision is made unilaterally by one spouse who says that he or she is leaving. At other times it is a decision that both spouses explore for themselves and then discuss together. There are a lot of issues spouses take into consideration when deciding about the future of their marriages, such as the love and regard they have for one another and the love and commitment they have to their children.

In both cases, Sherri and James and Jessica and Frank decided they wanted to work on their marriages. They faced considerable challenges—unique to each couple—but they chose to continue to invest in the marriages that they had been a part of for so many years. Other couples make the decision to separate or divorce.

RECOMMENDATIONS FOR COUPLES

I am not going to take a position on whether couples should divorce or reconcile following disclosure or discovery. There are many different views on divorce within Christian circles, so whenever possible I help couples make their decisions in light of what is taught in their faith community and in consultation with their pastor. In other words, the question of divorce is an important one, and it can only be made by the couple and in the context of pastoral counsel.

What I want to do is offer a few thoughts that couples might find helpful as they sort out the issues that arise. At times I may focus more on issues that come up for couples who have decided to work on their marriages, but some of these recommendations are important considerations regardless.

A Word to the Sexual-Minority Spouse

Describe attractions rather than identify with them. As you think about your relationship with your spouse, a good place to begin is with the distinction we have been making between same-sex attraction, a homosexual orientation, and a gay identity (chapter 2). Remember that at the most descriptive level, you experience same-sex attraction. In other words, your attractions do not necessarily signal your identity or define who you really are. It is more complicated than that.

When you label yourself, to some extent you are claiming a set of behaviors that correspond with your identity label. Instead of doing this, it may be helpful to use more descriptive language (for example, "I experience same-sex attraction") rather than forming an identity around your attractions by stating, "I am gay." Remember that although many people integrate their experiences of attraction into a gay identity, you can choose not to. Same-sex attraction doesn't have to be expressed or consolidated through sexual behavior. These are important decisions you face. But the use of descriptive language is particularly important to you as a couple if you decide you want to focus on reconciliation in the marriage.

Explore the question: What do these attractions mean? The next step is for you as the sexual minority (and to some extent your spouse) to try to better understand your attractions, including what they mean and where they came from. This is really a question of attributions, which are the connections people make between events and experiences in their lives. As we talked about with the three-tier distinction, many people believe that their attractions signal who they really are. In other words, to some, attractions are synonymous with identity. This answer to the question may sometimes lead a couple to separate or divorce. But equating attractions to identity may not be very helpful for couples who are committed to reconciliation.

The couples I know who have decided to stay together have often attributed same-sex attractions to the fall, not unlike so many other things that are essentially a cause for caution in a person's life. Another way the sexual minority might think about their attractions is that they are a result of experiences they had growing up. If so, this might be worth exploring further in ministry or in counseling. Perhaps paying attention to this will be helpful in dealing with the attractions more constructively. But the point is, you will need to sort out how to think about yourself in light of your attractions.

A related question: What weight do I give to other parts of who I am? Related to the question about attractions and their meanings is a question about how much weight to give to same-sex attractions in light of other things you know to be true about yourself as the sexual-minority spouse. Recall what we discussed in chapter 2; in addition to sexual attractions, you can reflect on

- your biological sex as male or female;
- your gender identity or how masculine or feminine you feel;
- what you intend to do with your attractions;
- what you have already done with your attractions;
- what you believe is right or wrong with respect to behavior and identity.

Most people do not give equal weight to these different facets of who they are, instead placing one or two of these things above the others. As we've mentioned, some sexual minorities see their same-sex attractions as the first and last word on their sense of who they are as a person. But others tend to see who they are in light of God making them male or female, or in light of their values and sense of identity in Christ. To them, their Christlikeness is more important and "real" than the other factors.

Can you align your behavior and identity with your beliefs and values? The term for this is *congruence,* which means harmony between what you believe and what you do. For the sexual-minority spouse, this idea of congruence may be tied to what you want in terms of your marriage. It may have to do with the love and emotional commitments you have made in your specific relationship, as well as other values associated with marriage in general. An example of congruence is when a spouse holds on to a covenantal view of marriage, and therefore decides to stay and work on the relationship with his or her partner in light of that covenant.

Working on sexual identity and what it means and how you will live in light of it will likely take some time. I have found that it generally takes about a year to really work through these issues in a way that gives you a sense of peace and confidence in the direction you are moving. It is also a time for you and your spouse to revisit what it means to build trust. This is something that was lost in light of what will feel like deception to your spouse. As you become increasingly transparent, you have an opportunity to be honest and in doing so to rebuild trust. This cannot be rushed. It takes time. If you are looking for accountability in this area (and I think that is important), I encourage you to find that through a local ministry, a self-help program, or a mutual aid support group that addresses sexuality-related concerns and sets you up with an accountability partner or sponsor.

For example, when I met with Sherri and James, I helped James develop a structure for reconciliation with Sherri. This structure involved sobriety from behaviors that undermined his goals for his marriage. He was involved in a local ministry and had an accountability partner there. He also attended a self-help group and had a sponsor there. He shared some of his concerns and received prayer and practical support from two to three close men in his life. He was also able to purchase software that placed a barrier between himself and images that he had made a habit of viewing but that he now wanted to say no to.

Wisely, Sherri did not function as James' accountability partner. If Sherri were to be in that role, she would not learn to trust James. After all, in an accountability role, she would be able to look over his shoulder, checking on everything she had questions about. Instead, she was able to create a space for trust to grow as she watched James participate fully in the framework for reconciliation in the marriage.

Although much of the information covered above is important for both you and your spouse, it is primarily directed at the sexual minority. Let's turn our attention now to the spouse of the sexual minority, as both partners would likely benefit from understanding the themes we discuss here.

A Word to the Spouse of the Sexual Minority

I mentioned above that, depending on the way in which disclosure or discovery occurred, there may be a real experience of betrayal or deception that is now part of the history of your mixed-orientation marriage. This experience of betrayal or other relationship offense has been described by psychologists as "interpersonal trauma."[3] Don't underestimate how important it is to carefully navigate through this trauma. I have found that many couples feel pressured (either from themselves or from others) to move on, to forgive quickly, and to get to a better place in their marriage. While I am a supporter of forgiveness in this context, I find that I have to slow people down a little. They need to work through how they feel about the relationship, how they feel about themselves, how they feel about their spouse, and so on, and all of this takes time.

This seems especially difficult for Christians. I suspect that they feel they must forgive, so they "white knuckle it" by claiming forgiveness in principle while their emotional experience (what they actually feel inside) lags far behind. It is okay to forgive in principle while you work through the emotions of forgiveness over time—as long as the emotional experience is not neglected. If the emotional experience is neglected or essentially pressed down or kept out of sight, it will come out sideways—perhaps down the road in the form of resentment or anger or depression or some other reaction that seems out of place.

I would say that it takes a minimum of one year to really work through interpersonal trauma related to an affair or a sense of relationship betrayal. Even in marriages in which there has been no actual physical affair—perhaps only same-sex fantasy and masturbation to pornography—the spouse of the sexual minority is still dealing with incredibly difficult information that feels like a betrayal of trust about *who each of them has been* in this marriage, as well as *who they are as a couple.*

The literature on working through interpersonal trauma suggests that the spouse who feels deceived typically works through the following stages: (1) impact, (2) a search for meaning, and (3) recovery.[4] The first stage, *impact*, refers to the initial realization of the effect of the offense on the marriage and on themselves as a person. This is similar to what I discussed above as a stage of discovery or disclosure, but it is perhaps tied more directly to how the betrayed spouse emotionally experiences the impact on themselves and their marriage, as they have a considerable stake in the relationship that seems to be threatened by this recent revelation.

The next stage is *a search for meaning*. This refers to the time in which the spouse is trying to understand what happened and why. If their partner has been having an affair, or if their partner has been viewing gay pornography, this is about trying to make sense of that.

For Sherri, the search for meaning meant understanding James' early experiences of attraction at a young age. This included his exposure to pornography at that time, and the way that looking at and fantasizing about such images became a strong habit and a behavior that helped soothe him, providing an outlet when he felt confused or angry or disappointed.

For Frank, the search for meaning was not as much of a driving force, but he was able to acknowledge that Jessica felt she had unmet emotional needs from childhood, and that her recent emotional pull to a woman was a reflection or expression of that.

The last stage is referred to as *recovery*. For those who are able to work though interpersonal trauma, this is the time when they use the new understanding they gained through their search for meaning in order to function better, as evidenced by moving beyond the pain and anger they felt before.

The recovery stage is also when most spouses make a decision about the future of their relationship. I mentioned above that often couples want to get to this point quickly, rushing forgiveness in an attempt to reconcile. This is dangerous because it underestimates the impact of the interpersonal trauma as it tries to take a shortcut through the process. Couples need time to get their bearings about what has happened and why, what it would mean to move forward, and what steps are a necessary part of the process.

It is also important to remember that there is not always reconciliation. Both spouses essentially reevaluate the relationship in light of current behavior and questions about identity and faithfulness. The decision the couple faces about their marriage is a very personal one, a decision that needs to be made by both spouses and in the context of pastoral care. Regardless of whether the couple works toward reconciliation or decides to divorce, it is helpful to keep these steps in mind, since working through interpersonal trauma sometimes means not being bound by the past pain and loss of a previous relationship.

RESILIENCE AND MIXED-ORIENTATION COUPLES

When a couple decides to stay together, I teach them about several important tools that can strengthen their relationship. These tools include communication, fostering a sense of "us," flexibility, and sexual intimacy.[5]

Communication: When and how to talk to one another

The *when* is easy to answer: frequently. It is important that couples talk to one another every day. This involves "checking in" on how each person is doing, what's going on that day, what's coming up, and the general ins and outs of life.

In addition to talking with your spouse, it's also good to have other people in your life that you can go to for honest conversations. Jessica identified a few key people she could talk to about her experiences, her work in counseling, and the challenges she faced in relationships. She could talk to Frank about that too, but she quickly identified a line between keeping him in the loop (i.e., letting him ask how she was doing, which was an act of care and intimacy) and turning to him for accountability per se. Again, by resisting the temptation to turn Frank into an accountability partner, Jessica was able to create a space in which Frank was able to learn to have confidence in the work Jessica was doing and thus grow in trust and intimacy.

Sherri and James' story was a little different. James was able to talk with Sherri about what he was doing, but Sherri struggled with anxiety about James and had a tendency to want to review Web site history and other "checks" against his sobriety, which would mean taking on the role of an accountability partner. But eventually she learned to trust that James was taking the right steps toward reconciliation in their marriage since he was in counseling and a small group, and had a sponsor and an accountability partner. Of course, even within this framework, there is no guarantee against more deception. But that is the nature of trust-building. What makes it difficult is that if there is no risk, there is no opportunity to trust. What seems critical is to identify a counselor who can help you as a couple to create a framework that lends itself to the development and expression of trust and trustworthiness, and then work closely with both of you throughout the process.

In addition to the quantity of communication, the quality is also important. Honesty, for example, is crucial. But the communication should also be characterized by empathy. Can each person empathize with the other? This means hearing the other person and understanding what they are saying from their point of view.

Right after disclosure, as you work on your marriage, most of the communication may be about issues like grief and loss, sexuality and behavior. These conversations are appropriate and even necessary, and they don't mean the spouse is functioning as an accountability partner. I encourage this kind of honesty about the struggles being faced. That said, the details of temptations, setbacks, and related concerns should be reserved for the accountability partner who is walking this out with the sexual-minority spouse.

What this suggests is that the sexual minority spouse needs to have in his or her life a group of people who are working toward the same goal as the sexual minority. These people might include a small group or ministry support, an accountability partner, a counselor, a pastor, and a couple of friends who are aware of what is going on and can check in to provide encouragement and support.

A sense of "us"

There are many ways to grow or cultivate a sense of togetherness, or a sense of "us," in your relationship again.[6] For some people, this begins by reviewing why you as a couple got together in the first place; in other words, what drew you to one another? What were some of your early shared experiences? How did you first grow together as a couple?

It can also be helpful to review what you currently enjoy that is helping you stay together. You not only had a sense of yourself as a couple initially, you also have one now—what are you enjoying together that gives you a shared sense of identity?

It can also be beneficial for some couples to reflect on their shared identity as believers. This means reflecting on the covenant they made and what that means to each of them.

For Jessica and Frank, a discussion of their sense of "us" quickly led to a discussion of who they were as parents and how they had poured themselves into the lives of their children. Their sense of identity as parents was very important to both of them. We didn't want to limit their sense of identity as "us" to their role as parents, but it was something they both genuinely valued, which made it worthwhile to discuss and consider. They also had a shared sense of identity as Christians and as people who were active in their community and in their local church. Lastly, they both expressed an interest in enhancing their sense of "us" through sexual intimacy, which I will discuss more below.

Staying flexible

Flexibility is another quality found in couples that are able to stay together and grow in their appreciation for each other and their marriage. Rather than using examples from other marriages or from the media or entertainment as a standard against which they measure themselves, they adapt to who they are and the relationship that is their own. For them it is helpful to see their marriage as something unique that each of them has decided to pour themselves into.

Addressing intimacy

Often one of the areas of anxiety for couples in mixed-orientation relationships is sexual intimacy. For couples who decide to stay together, I encourage them to see their time of sexual intimacy as something that is uniquely their own. It is important not to compare themselves to other couples or to images or messages from entertainment or the broader culture; rather, they are building something unique that is a reflection of who they are as a couple.

Let me close by returning to Jessica and Frank one last time. When I started to counsel them in the area of sexual intimacy, we discussed the anxiety each felt about whether to directly address this topic. Jessica feared sex "wouldn't compare" and that their failure would lead to despair and erase all the gains they had made. Frank struggled to talk about sex in marriage at all, reflecting the pressure many men feel to have all the answers. After listening to and working through some of their concerns, we agreed to proceed with trying to enhance sexual intimacy. They learned how to focus on their own experience of intimacy rather than making comparisons to others. We then reviewed what is normal and to be expected when it comes to sexual response. We talked about the differences between initiating, responsive, and principled desires. *Initiating* desire has to do with a drive or interest in pursuing sex in marriage. *Responsive* desire has more to do with a spouse responding favorably to sex once they feel connected to their partner. *Principled* desire is more like what Christians do in their spiritual lives when they don't feel like spending time with God: they choose to do it anyway, recognizing that it is a good thing for the relationship. In the area of sexual intimacy, principled desire is kind of like that. A spouse may work on the sexual aspect of the marriage even if he or she doesn't currently feel a strong initiating desire or a strong responsive desire.

Jessica and Frank also completed exercises that helped them with communication in general and in the area of sexual intimacy in particular. They began reading the book *A Celebration of Sex,* by Doug Rosenau, and discussed the chapters and their applications to them as a couple. I assigned other specific exercises to enhance intimacy and improve communication further. These were followed by discussions of technique while also processing emotional reactions to each exercise, keeping in mind realistic, modest expectations for what they would create together.

CONCLUSION

When a spouse's same-sex attraction or behavior is either announced or discovered, it is a life-altering experience for both the sexual minority and the spouse. There are many obstacles facing mixed-orientation couples, not the least of which is the question of whether to continue in the marriage. It can be helpful to realize that couples in this situation go through identifiable stages, as this lets them understand that what they feel and experience is to be expected. Also, to the extent that there is interpersonal trauma, this can be addressed regardless of whether a couple decides to stay together or not. The decision about the future of the marriage should be made in the context of mature, discerning pastoral care.

TAKE-HOME POINTS

- If your spouse discloses a gay identity, or his or her same-sex attractions or behavior are discovered, give yourself time to process the range of emotions that accompany such disclosure.

- Keep in mind the four stages that are associated with discovery: *awareness, emotional response, acceptance of reality,* and *negotiating a future.*

- Remember the three-tier distinction and use descriptive language to discuss feelings of attraction.

- Working through interpersonal trauma involves dealing with *impact, a search for meaning,* and *recovery.*

- For couples who decide to work on their marriage, important tools include communication, fostering a sense of "us," flexibility, and sexual intimacy.

PART THREE
QUESTIONS FOR THE CHURCH

CHAPTER EIGHT

Whose People Are We Talking About?

A few years ago I sat in on a session at the American Psychological Association (APA) on religious people who were conflicted about their sexual identity. The presenters and the moderator were all gay psychologists, and each spoke of how they, as members of the gay community, had failed their own people, driving them away from the gay community and into the arms of the conservative religious community. They were genuinely bothered by this. They truly felt that they had failed "their people," sending them to a group that, in their minds, took advantage of them and misrepresented research to the detriment of sexual minorities.

Although I disagreed with their conclusions, it was enlightening to hear gay psychologists speak of the Christians I saw in counseling as having more in common with themselves than with me.

It got me thinking about why the church doesn't lead with the thought and attitude that Christians who struggle with homosexuality are *our people*. Think about that for a second: Sexual minorities in the church, by which I mean believers who experience same-sex attraction, are *our people*. Framing the issue this way can lead to greater compassion as the church tries to find ways to provide support and encouragement to those in our own communities who would benefit from it.

I don't think Christians who are sexual minorities feel like they are part of "us." The nature of their struggle is tremendously isolating, and there is so much shame involved in it. Shame is different from guilt. *Guilt* is about feeling bad for something you've done. *Shame* is about feeling bad for who you are. Because sexuality is tied to our sense of ourselves as a person, it is common for the Christian who experiences same-sex attraction to feel shame for their experience, regardless of their behavior.[1]

What's the result? Often Christians who struggle in this way don't feel they are part of the Christian community. They often play the same tape over and over in their heads: they don't belong; they aren't good enough; people would reject them if they knew what was really going on; and so on. This can be traced back to shame.

But in addition to their internal struggles, they might also receive the message from others that they would not be welcomed. Few churches reach out to the Christian who is a sexual minority, even if that person is what we might refer to as a "sincere struggler."[2] The sincere struggler is the believer who is genuinely trying to live faithfully before God with their sexuality. In other words, they agree with traditional Christian doctrine about sexuality and sexual behavior; they recognize that full sexual expression is reserved for marriage between a man and a woman. In fact, they value this expression and in many cases want it for themselves. But they often struggle with whether a heterosexual marriage is attainable.

I want to contrast the sincere struggler with the "assertive advocate." This is the Christian sexual minority who advocates for a change in Christian doctrine about sexuality and sexual behavior. He or she leads with advocacy, often placing great pressure on the local church or denomination to change policies that have long been part of a Judeo-Christian understanding of sexuality.

The sincere struggler and the assertive advocate share some things in common. Obviously, both experience same-sex attraction. Both are believers. Both are trying to be part of a local community of faith. But they approach the topic in different ways, with different emphases and ways of relating to fellow believers. Also, sincere strugglers can become assertive advocates after years of frustraions with the local church, their own same-sex sexuality, or other issues. Later in this chapter and in the next chapter I will offer suggestions on how to relate to both kinds of believers, in part because it is important not to confuse the two or respond to all people as though they were delivering the same message.

MISTAKEN IDENTITY

Back to the question from the title of this chapter: Whose people are we talking about? The gay community admits they have failed to embrace sexual minority Christians, and few churches are welcoming them, so where do they go? And what do they want? To explore these questions, it is important to find out how same-sex-attracted Christians see their own identities. What do they say about themselves?

The experience I had at the APA session was repeated recently. I was watching the trailer to *Equality U*, a documentary of the first year of Equality Ride, a social justice event by the gay activist group Soulforce. One of the leaders of Equality Ride stated, "We say to all the students who are suffering in the closet that God loves you and that God affirms you without reservation."[3] He was speaking to Christians who were sexual minorities on Christian campuses, who he believed were closeted and in need of the specific kinds of changes he was recommending. He was telling the campuses to embrace homosexuality and homosexual behavior as a blessing from God, a good to be enjoyed and celebrated by the Christian community.

There are certainly some students on Christian college campuses who privately identify as gay but would prefer to publicly identify as gay, wishing their campus policies would change. They may have chosen to go to a traditional Christian college because no one knew about their same-sex attractions or their desire to live out a gay identity. Or perhaps their parents sent them there. However, I was recently involved in a study[4] of Christian sexual minorities at three Christian colleges, and we did not find this experience to be very common. Instead, most students appeared to support and adhere to their campus policies regarding the place of sex in heterosexual marriage.

In other words, *Equality U* portrays sexual-minority Christians as isolated and seeking freedom. Yet in our research, Christian sexual minorities seemed to support a traditional Christian sexual ethic. This may change over time, of course, especially as younger people are exposed to the gay script. Recall how we defined the gay script in chapter 3:

- Same-sex attractions signal a naturally occurring or "intended by God" distinction between homosexuality, heterosexuality, and bisexuality.

- Same-sex attractions signal who you really are as a person (emphasis on *discovery*).

- Same-sex attractions are at the core of who you are as a person.

- Same-sex behavior is an extension of that core.

- Self-actualization of your sexual identity is crucial for your fulfillment.

I also shared that this is a very compelling script to a young person who is sorting out what to make of their attraction to the same sex. They may see the gay script as a realistic account of their experience and an intuitive way to resolve potential conflicts with their Christian upbringing.

But at this point we did not see this in very many of the students. The Christian sexual minorities who completed our survey seemed to value the very teachings that Equality Ride said were oppressive to them. Very few adopted a gay identity for themselves. In fact, they tended to think of themselves more as Christians than as gay. This was similar to other studies we have conducted of Christians who are sexual minorities: While some integrate their experience of same-sex attraction into a gay identity (and the people and institutions that support a gay identity), many choose not to. Rather, they form their identity around Christ or some other part of who they are as a person. But forming an identity in Christ is typically a prominent theme among those who do not embrace a gay identity.

Returning to Christian college students, what the sexual minorities we surveyed wanted was to be on a campus that felt more supportive of them. We had several questions about campus climate for sexual minorities, and they shared the challenges they faced. Generally, the campuses were not easy places to experience this struggle with sexual identity. It wasn't that the policies were oppressive; again, sexual minorities seemed to support the policies and the theological foundations underneath them. Rather, they struggled at times with the climate, more specifically how the climate was shaped by derogatory statements from other students. They didn't hear these comments from faculty or staff; this negative atmosphere was usually found in the residence halls rather than the classrooms.

Imagine if you experienced same-sex attraction and heard your friends talking negatively about gays or using derogatory terms as put-downs. It would be hard to see those same friends as safe people with whom to share your struggle.

But let me return to the main point: We seem to have a case of mistaken identity. Activists continue to misunderstand or fail to accurately portray the very people they are attempting to help. Christians who are sexual minorities may often choose traditional Christian colleges and universities because they share the values that are reflected in those institution's policies. They are not secretly hoping to be freed from these policies; rather, they want the institutions themselves to be places in which they can be more transparent about their experiences and receive more support in the context of their struggles. But why aren't our Christian colleges and universities more supportive?

A LESSON LEARNED

When I was preparing to launch our survey of sexual minorities on Christian college campuses, I had a meeting with many leaders of Christian colleges. There was definitely enthusiasm; such a survey hadn't been done before, and most knew that the topic was important. The buzz that was created led to about a dozen schools expressing interest in the project. I thought that was a great start. However, as we got closer to the launch date and needed to get firm commitments about which schools would participate, the number dwindled quickly. Christian colleges were not prepared to survey sexual minorities on their campuses.

In fact, I recall speaking by phone to one college president the day before the study was to be launched. He said he knew the topic was important, and he believed it was a good idea to conduct the study. He even wanted to possibly participate in the future. . . . However, he shared that it would be too difficult to do it now. Parents and board members would just not understand why we were interested in homosexuality.

I tried to explain to him something that I had never before put into words: "These students on our campuses are our people. They are Christians. They are sorting out important questions about their sexual identity and behavior, and we need to have a better understanding of their experiences so that we can identify better ways to provide them with support."

I went on to share what would happen if we did not do this kind of research: "There are other organizations out there that will force the issue. Other groups will make claims about our students and what they experience and what they want. But we have an opportunity to ask the questions that matter to us and to our communities. . . ."

Click. Well, it didn't end that abruptly, but the phone call did end. And that college did not participate. Most of the Christian colleges that had previously expressed enthusiasm and support for the project did not participate. Only three of the twelve did.

This process helped me clarify the question "Whose people are we talking about?" I have been to many Christian colleges and universities over the past ten years. I can tell you that young people today are expecting better things from the church on the topic of homosexuality. They are growing up with good friends and family members who are gay. They want to elevate the discussion about homosexuality. They want to see that their faith has something to say about this controversial topic. They want to be relevant.

I think part of what makes it difficult is that they see the church as either silent on the topic or as pushing a view they do not understand or agree with. The view they oppose doesn't have to do with what the Bible says about homosexuality. Rather, they disagree with the focus being on causation and change. They are troubled by statements that homosexuality is caused by nothing but _____, and that homosexuality can be easily changed. The "nothing but _____" sometimes refers to childhood sexual abuse and sometimes to strained parent-child relationships, but regardless of which cause is pushed, they see these easy explanations as missing something that is important. They also don't buy the strong claims about change. After all, if sexual orientation were so easy to change, wouldn't most, if not all, people who did not like their homosexual orientation simply make the choices that would lead to a dramatic and fundamental change?

THE REAL ISSUE: SUPPORTING OUR PEOPLE

Questions about causation and change are important. They are challenging. They are relevant questions for Christians in our culture today. But Christians should start with an understanding of Scripture, an understanding of God's revealed will regarding all matters, including matters of sexuality and its expression. In this way, science, while informative and instructive, will not be trump. So while the cause and change debates are interesting to some, they are not the defining issues for the Christian.

Let me say it plainly one more time: The traditional Christian sexual ethic does not hinge on the causes of sexual attraction or orientation.

Also: The traditional Christian sexual ethic does not hinge on whether or not sexual orientation can change.

Well-meaning Christians want easy answers to these two difficult questions because they have trouble understanding why people suffer with enduring conditions. We will talk about this more in chapter 9. But I think by focusing so much energy and attention on these two issues, the church has actually provided little by way of instruction or guidance or pastoral care to those Christians who are sexual minorities. The message I think they hear from many churches today is *God hates you. You need to change.*

What the assertive advocate does is take this experience and demand changes to the church that are so radical they are not recognizable in Christian history. They want the church to affirm that same-sex behavior is good, and that it should embrace homosexuality as an expression of God's diverse plan for human sexuality and its expression.

But there is another way. Without compromising its position on the issue of same-sex behavior, the church can recognize that Christians who are sexual minorities are our people, and we can speak to them. Providing support and pastoral care to the sincere struggler will take one form while supportive pastoral care to the assertive advocate will take another.

Unfortunately, sincere strugglers are not organized in the same way as assertive advocates. They are often silenced, marginalized by both the Christian community and the gay community. The Christian community often tells them that if they don't experience a change in their attractions, they aren't living faithfully before God. Meanwhile, the gay community may mock them, treating them as though they—by virtue of being strugglers—are suppressing their sexuality, their "true nature," and therefore doing further harm to the gay community. So even here the script tells sexual-minority Christians that their first and primary obligation is to the gay community.

In contrast, the church should tell the sexual-minority Christian that their first and primary obligation is to God, to the person of Jesus Christ, and to becoming Christlike. After speaking this truth, churches should follow it up with a meaningful way to support sexual minorities through the process. If our only message is that through enough effort and faith they will become heterosexual, we are misleading them. We mislead them by setting the wrong standard for what counts as success.

Heterosexuality is not the measure of success for the Christian sexual minority. What matters is Christlikeness, regardless of whether sexual attractions change significantly.[5]

What the Christian community can offer the Christian sexual minority is a vision for what it means to be Christlike. That vision places the Christian sexual minority squarely in the middle of the Christian community. *They* become *us*. We are all supposed to be working toward the same goal. Whether we experience same-sex attraction or not, we are all to move toward Christlikeness.

A church that facilitates this kind of community treats all people with respect. Such a church avoids negative comments about the gay community. The pastoral leadership takes a lead with wording and language here. They set a tone when they talk about people who are sorting out sexual identity concerns. This kind of church welcomes broken people and relies on the Holy Spirit to work in the lives of those who listen to the Word of God preached and lived by those in the congregation.

A church that facilitates this kind of community avoids "arrogant optimism" and replaces it with "realistic biblical hope."[6] The former refers to the tendency within the church to offer platitudes and assurances without sitting with people in their suffering or confusion. The latter, realistic biblical hope, retains optimism about who we are and what our future is, while recognizing that requests for help may be answered by God in ways we either don't expect or don't want, since He has a different perspective than we do on what is needed.

A church that fosters this kind of community does not shame

people who continue to struggle. Instead, they have a realistic biblical hope. In other words, they know that people may make strides in a certain direction, but those gains are often followed by setbacks. If the church overreacts to struggles or setbacks with shame, it can drive people away from the church and into isolation, or it can lead them to misrepresent their progress as they are afraid to reveal what's really going on in their lives.

We turn our attention now to a different point of emphasis in the discussion about change. We want to take a look at the potential benefits of exploring the meaning and practical application of an identity in Christ.

HOW "CHANGE" REALLY WORKS

This is essentially a practical theology of sanctification.[7] To Christians, sanctification means being made holy. Another phrase often used to describe sanctification is to be "set apart" for God's purposes ("set apart" is the definition of "holy"). There have been many Christians throughout history who have taken control of their internal and external lives and are "faithfully dealing with their desires for the same sex according to the plain teaching of Scripture."[8] In other words, they have chosen not to embrace homosexual behavior in spite of their same-sex attractions. For those considering this path, it is important to understand that not only are they not alone in their struggles, but that God can use these circumstances as a means by which He can provide grace and mercy.

Sanctification is not simply a matter of denying yourself pleasure or enjoyment. That is not an accurate way to frame this from a Christian perspective. It involves seeing things in relation to their ultimate purpose and value in light of the kingdom and economy of God.

The assertive advocate might raise the red flag: "There goes another Christian promising the rewards of a future life but denying the pleasures of this life." But, again, that is not a Christian understanding of the circumstances the believer faces. As C. S. Lewis notes, the fact that heaven awaits the Christian is not "simply tacked on to the activity" of obedient living, for example, but rewards are "the activity itself in consummation."[9] In other words, the activity of being sanctified is a reward here and now, not just for the afterlife. He writes:

> Those who have attained everlasting life in the vision of God doubtless know very well that it is no mere bribe, but the very consummation of their earthly discipleship; but we who have not yet attained it cannot know this in the same way, and cannot even begin to know it at all except by continuing to obey and finding the reward of our obedience in our increasing power to desire the ultimate reward.[10]

The Christian looks seriously at both the activity and its end result. For the Christian, our activity is obedience, discipleship, and sanctification. That is, being made more and more in the likeness of Christ. And the final result of this is to be fully Christlike in the glorification that awaits us in heaven.

I remember listening to John Piper elaborate on this point in a talk he gave on the immeasurable power of grace.[11] What he said is that we were "made for the glory of God's grace." Our inheritance is "to spend eternity giving glory to God." If the church doesn't teach that, we run the risk of relying on heterosexuality as the ultimate goal, or as the measure of the sexual minority's spiritual maturity.

We also run the risk of treating praise as a means to an end, when praise is the end in and of itself. The church doesn't teach sexual minorities to praise God to receive heterosexuality in exchange. ("I praise you so I can become heterosexual.") Praise is the goal. It is the end, not the means to an end.

If this sounds foreign to our ears, it may be that we have been too influenced by our culture, one that would see such a discussion as antiquated and too far removed from our emphasis today on self-actualization. We may do well to reflect on how we should form a Christian worldview on matters of identity and behavior. This is not just theoretical, it is practical.

I was recently watching a DVD in a series by Ray Vanderlaan titled *When the Rabbi Says Come.* Ray was sharing a little background on what it meant to be a disciple of Jesus, including how there were rigorous standards for being a disciple of a rabbi in Jesus' day. It was a tremendous privilege and honor reserved only for those who had the acumen and the passion for it. When disciples would sit under the teaching of a rabbi, they were really saying that they wanted to *be like the rabbi* (in their knowledge of sacred texts, in their spiritual life, in their character, and so on). Most people were not selected to be disciples of a rabbi; most went back to following their family trade. Jesus turned this upside down by seeking out disciples and inviting them to follow Him. Jesus' invitation is an invitation to all Christians, all followers of Christ, to identify with Him, to follow Him, and to become like Him.

In some ways this forms the basis for the question Dallas Willard, a Christian writer and philosopher, raises in what he refers to as a "curriculum of Christ-likeness."[12] In Willard's way of thinking, the question is not "What would Jesus do?" but "How did Jesus live?"

Such a curriculum involves two important practices. The first is "Clearly positioning the context before the heavenly Father's present rule through Jesus."[13] In other words, acknowledging that God is in charge changes everything. It enables us to see our circumstances accurately and from a Christian perspective, which means in the context of God's redemptive plan. Sometimes it is hard to see struggles with same-sex attraction from that perspective. This is especially true since the competing script, the gay script mentioned in chapter 2, is quite compelling, often making it that much more difficult to see things clearly.

The second important practice in a curriculum of Christlikeness involves "Walking the individual through actual cases in their own lives to give them experienced-based understanding and assurance."[14] This means that learning a curriculum is not an intellectual endeavor, or at least it does not only involve our intellect. Real-life application has to occur. Individuals have to work out in their own lives the very reality of who Christ is and how their identity and lives are shaped by Him.

It is also important for us to be in relationships with one another in which we are able to be transparent. What often makes this difficult is the isolation sexual minorities feel because of shame. As we mentioned before, they often feel that there is something inherently wrong with them or that they would not be loved and accepted if people really knew what they were going through. But we are to walk alongside the person who experiences same-sex attraction, just as they walk alongside us in our spiritual lives. We share and encourage one another as we grow closer to God and more in the image and likeness of His Son.

Note that the appeal to spiritual disciplines is not to change orientation as such, but instead to help us live a life and form an identity in a way that is otherwise impossible for anyone. Spiritual disciplines are "practices that change the inner self and its relationship to the 'helper' [*Holy Spirit*], so that we actually can do what we would and avoid what we would not."[15] This seems very much consistent with our discussion and emphasis on sexual identity.

This brings us to the work of the Holy Spirit. If all of us are attempting to apply Willard's advice here, the function of the Holy Spirit appears to be "to move within our souls, and especially our minds, to present the person of Jesus and the reality of his kingdom."[16] Put differently, the Holy Spirit is active and plays a vital role in shaping our inner lives and the acts that come to reflect the nature of our inner lives.

Do you see how our language has changed? We are no longer talking about Christians with same-sex attractions as though they were in a unique category of people trying to live faithfully before God. Yes, there are unique challenges associated with same-sex sexuality in a culture like ours and in light of the prominence of the gay script. But we do well to speak as fellow travelers on a journey toward the same destination.

This approach is nothing new. It is consistent with what the church has historically taught about self-discipline. This perspective obviously means looking to the future. If this world is all there is, then an approach that incorporates self-discipline wouldn't make sense. But it wouldn't make sense for any of us. And to the extent that Christians end up shaped by our culture and living just like nonbelievers around us, we may be guilty of putting a burden on sexual minorities that the rest of us do not accept for ourselves. So this is an area in which all Christians can make strides and in which those who do not struggle with sexual identity issues can take the lead.

If people see their lives laid before them—in the present life and in the future, both of which are properly understood as the kingdom of God—then we will live in hope for tomorrow and with access to resources in our spiritual lives today. We will anticipate God re-forming the world and ourselves, and this will have immediate relevance to how we live in the present.[17]

I mentioned above that it is important to listen to the voices of those Christians who are sorting out these issues in their own lives. A few years ago I began a series of studies of Christians who experienced same-sex attraction. We contacted gay-affirming churches, and we also contacted conservative religious ministries.

Some of the participants embraced a gay identity; others chose not to identify as gay. It was humbling to come to a better understanding of both groups; I had no idea at that time where this line of research would take me.

The first group was making a departure from traditional Christian doctrine about sexuality and sexual behavior. They seemed aware of this. They believed that being gay was who they really were, and that they could only be authentic if they were true to themselves as gay persons. They lived out the discovery metaphor I mentioned in chapter 2. Some might say that they previously denied who they were, or that they tried to change, but that they came to the realization of who they really were: gay. To this group of Christians, they thought of "being gay" as part of God's plan. To get to a place of congruence, they needed to change their understanding of Scripture to correspond with their identity and behavior.

The other group of Christians we studied seemed to begin and end with their religious beliefs and values about homosexuality. They did not experience homosexuality as who they really were; many thought of it as an expression of the fall, much like some people are susceptible to diabetes or cancer or depression or anxiety or alcoholism.[18] In framing the issue this way, they rejected the discovery metaphor.

This second group seemed to be saying that while part of the diversity we see in nature appears to reflect God's creativity, other aspects of what we see and experience in nature appear to reflect the fall—a distortion of that diversity. What was really important to this group was living in God's will. For them, same-sex behavior did not reflect God's intention for sexual expression. So forming a gay identity around attractions that led to homosexual behavior would not be good. This group was what I've been referring to as "sincere strugglers."

For these Christians, what are the obstacles to pursuing a deeper life in Christ? The gay community can be an obstacle when it tries to get them to embrace a gay identity by providing a script that sanctions and fosters a pattern of behavior of serious concern for the believer.

But the church can also be an obstacle if it pushes a simplistic expectation of change, by which I mean the expectation of a complete and categorical switch from homosexuality to heterosexuality as though it were the direct result of putting forth enough effort or having sufficient faith.

Both of these messages can move the believer away from their true purpose and stewardship, which means living responsibly with whatever has been entrusted to you. Stewardship is less of a "quick fix" than the other two messages, which can make it unattractive at first. The gay script is compelling because it often initially fits with a person's experience, or at least how they would like their experience to be. The emphasis on complete change is compelling too. When change occurs, there is great joy; but when it doesn't happen, it can become an obstacle to the Christian and his or her primary purpose of praising God. Stewardship, on the other hand, is difficult but extremely rewarding in the long run.

The challenge for the church is to support and equip and train Christians, *all* Christians, in meaningful ways. We do this together.

What the Church Should Avoid

In thinking about the sincere struggler, it can be wise to avoid several conscious or subconscious actions.

Avoid "tunnel vision." The church would do well to avoid focusing exclusively on homosexuality to the exclusion of other concerns. The people I know who are sorting this out are acutely sensitive to what looks like hypocrisy in the church—giving some sins a pass while focusing intently on other sins. To aid in this, consider discussing homosexuality only in the context of a broader discussion of a theology of human sexuality, including creation, the fall, redemption, glorification, and a discussion of both married and single sexuality.

The passage from Romans 1:26–27 comes to mind. While it is an important passage in which Paul uses homosexuality to illustrate a point, he also goes on to discuss sins of the mind, such as envy, covetousness, strife, pride, being unmerciful, and so on (v. 29–30). These are much more common struggles in the local church, and we want to remember that these should all be addressed in the life of the believer who is in the process of sanctification.

Avoid "boxing in." Keep the three-tier distinction in mind. Recognize the differences between attractions, orientation, and a gay identity. What we don't want to do is box people in by prematurely labeling those who do not fit neatly into what we think masculinity or femininity should look like in our social circles. This will only make it more difficult for them to find safe people to talk to about their experiences. If someone experiences same-sex attractions, give them space to *describe* their experiences rather than *identify* with them. If people label themselves prematurely, it may be helpful to introduce the three-tier distinction to see to what extent it resonates with them and their experiences.

Avoid "raising the bar." This means we want to avoid holding out expectations that are too high regarding healing or change. We don't want to communicate that someone has to be healed or changed to heterosexuality to have a testimony about what God is doing in their lives. What about the process? Let's encourage testimonies of how God is working day by day. This will mean revisiting how churches discuss and program around singles. Indeed, the topic of homosexuality and singleness is related in an important way. If the church has a low opinion of singles, then the church will imply the need for the Christian struggling with homosexuality to become heterosexual.

In contrast, when churches value being single not as a stage to "get through" but as a good state to be in, they can provide a place that is valued and meaningful to the Christian who is also a sexual minority. There are many more single heterosexual Christians than there are Christians who are sexual minorities. The church is in desperate need of speaking a meaningful word into what it means to be single in the church today.[19] The more we value being single, the more we will value the Christian sexual minority and be able to cast a vision for what it means to live a deep, rich, and fulfilling spiritual life.

Avoid "preaching to the choir." What I mean by this is that we need to do less preaching against homosexuality and more equipping of all believers to grow in a curriculum of Christlikeness. Equipping is going to be far more important in the years to come than preaching.

A few years ago we started a campaign at the Institute I direct. It is called Coming Alongside. The primary themes or tenets of the Coming Alongside campaign are to:

- Recognize the value in all people as image-bearers of God.
- Stand together with fellow believers who are sorting out sexual identity concerns.
- Remove the stigma often associated with the struggle itself.
- Encourage brothers and sisters in Christ who are trying to live faithfully before God.

There are important steps we can take as a Christian community. There is a need to speak into the lives of those believers who are sorting out these issues. But we are also speaking into our own lives. We are growing ourselves, working toward the same goal of obedience and Christlikeness.

The church also needs to find constructive ways to respond to the assertive advocate. I can think of no better resource available to the Christian community than Andrew Marin's book *Love Is an Orientation*.[20] No, it won't settle matters of church policy, but it can help improve discussions with those who are more assertive in their advocacy of homosexual behavior.

Marin offers open-ended questions that can help "elevate the conversation" with the gay community. For example, when asked, "Do you think homosexuality is a sin?"[21]—a question that is invariably on the mind of people on both sides of the debate—Marin encourages us to find common ground in our shared humanity, our shared experience of the fall. He offers another question for us to discuss with the assertive advocate: "What does it mean to you that such a perfect God still wants to be in relationship with imperfect beings such as us?"[22]

When asked, "Do you think someone can be gay *and* Christian?"[23] Marin offers the following: "What does the term 'gay Christian' mean to you and how has that impacted your life?"[24]

Similar open-ended questions are offered in response to questions about the causes of homosexuality and whether it can be changed, as well as questions about the eternal destination of members of the gay community. These are important questions to address in real relationships within the church community. They are important questions for both the sincere struggler and the assertive advocate, but often the assertive advocate is using these questions to advance an agenda that may be beyond what a faith community can manage. Often such advocacy, once understood, can be traced back to painful dealings and experiences within the church. Other times it appears to genuinely reflect a formed judgment that the advocate has reached and now feels would benefit the church and broader culture.

Advocacy for changes in church doctrine may become so heated or divisive that things become difficult for both the community and the assertive advocate, and a painful decision might have to be made to go in different directions. However, such steps should only be taken after great consideration and after many attempts have been made to have a civil dialogue about these issues.

BRING YOUR LIGHT

I was told this story by a pastor several years ago, and I think it applies to our discussion:

> A nobleman in the 1800s wondered what his legacy would be. He wanted to leave something behind that would speak to what was most important. He decided he would build a church. Of course, this took a long time, but when it was done, he felt that he had something that would be his legacy. The townspeople came to celebrate the completed church. In time, however, one of the onlookers noticed what looked like a fatal flaw. There were no lamps. How would this beautiful church be lit? There were brackets in the wall, holders for lamps, but no lamps.
>
> Then the nobleman gave each family a lamp. They were to bring the lamp every time they came to worship. "When you are here," he said, "it will be lighter. When you are not, it will be darker. Realize that when you are not here some part of God's house will be darkened."

I would like to see the church say to the sincere strugglers, "Bring your light." I don't think we think about Christian sexual minorities in this way. Yet I have been impressed by the depth of spiritual conviction I've seen among those Christians who are stewards of their sexuality. While I may get a pass in the areas I struggle with in life, these fellow believers face a hard decision every day. They say no to what the gay community and broader culture promotes so that they can say yes to something else, something they feel God is calling them to, even if they get little to no support from their local faith community.

I want to say to the Christians who are stewarding their sexuality: *Bring your light.* I recognize the stigma associated with this experience or struggle in particular. So be aware of that as you identify who you share your experience with. And keep in mind that the church will expect you to bring liberal theology to pressure the church to change its doctrine on sex. There will be fears that come with transparency.

Even with all of that, I want to say this: In time . . . share your experiences anyway.

TAKE-HOME POINTS

- Challenge yourself to see believers who are sorting out sexual identity questions as "your people," part of your community of faith.

- Recognize differences between assertive advocates and sincere strugglers—these differences will help you respond to people in both groups.

- Christian sexual minorities have the potential to grow tremendously in their spiritual lives, primarily because of what is gained in perseverance and character.

CHAPTER NINE

What Is the Church's Response to Enduring Conditions?

Terry came to see me about his struggle with homosexuality. He was a Christian in a mixed-orientation marriage. He had had several same-sex encounters throughout his marriage, often on business trips, and had recently come out to his wife, of almost twenty years, Linda. Both of them wanted to work things out to save their marriage. After all, they had been together for many years and had three children, ages sixteen, fourteen, and eleven.

The reason Terry came out to Linda was because he contracted HIV. He felt she needed to know, so he somehow found the words to tell her about his HIV status as well as his long-standing struggle with homosexuality. He confessed what he believed were his sins, particularly his sexual behaviors that placed both his and his wife's health at such great risk. Linda came to forgive him over time but was facing her own struggles. She had been diagnosed with cancer.

It was interesting to hear Terry talk about their different experiences with their besetting conditions. A besetting condition is an ongoing or enduring battle, whether it's against a disease, a temptation, an addiction, or something else. It is not something quickly or easily resolved, treated, or cured. Linda was able to share her struggle with cancer with her family, her co-workers, her girlfriends, her small group, and her large church. They rallied around her. They loved on her. They provided Linda with prayer support, meals for the family, time off from work, words of encouragement, and so much more. It was humbling to the family to receive such tangible expressions of love and support.

Despite all the prayer Linda received, she was not miraculously cured of her cancer. She received treatment for it, and it went into remission. But she lives her life with the awareness that it is part of her experience, a part of her history that shapes her future. The other Christians at Linda's church and in her small group believed that God could heal her of her cancer, and that's how they prayed. But the church did not blame Linda when she didn't experience a miraculous healing.

Terry's experience was dramatically different. He has not been able to tell many people about his HIV. No one at work knows. His children do not know. He has only shared his struggle with homosexuality with about four friends over the years. His small group does not know, and yet they pray for one another weekly. Needless to say, his church community does not know. He may be forced one day to share his HIV status if his health deteriorates, but he and his wife are waiting as long as possible. The stigma is too great to bear.

Obviously, Terry and his wife's diseases were contracted in very different ways. Linda's health condition is a result of forces beyond her control, while Terry's health condition is a direct result of his own behavior. And the gulf that separates Terry and Linda in terms of the support the church is providing is tremendous.

There is another difference between Terry's enduring condition and his wife's. In fact, to some extent Terry has two enduring conditions: his ongoing same-sex attractions and his HIV. Terry's HIV is a physical condition, not unlike his wife's cancer. His same-sex attraction, on the other hand, is a condition that leads to temptation to sin. We can all relate to experiencing besetting temptations in our lives, whether it's toward lust, greed, pride, or something else. Often besetting conditions are harder for us to talk about than our physical conditions.

I should add that Terry has prayed for healing from his same-sex attraction. Despite his prayers and the prayer support of his closest friends, his attractions to other men persist. Is he doing something wrong? I don't think so. But it's a question that is often asked about homosexuality yet rarely about cancer.

My experience with churches is that they can sometimes blame the person who contends with homosexuality for not trying hard enough or not having enough faith if their same-sex attractions persist. The message we are sending is that Terry must experience a dramatic change in sexual orientation to have a testimony of what God is doing in his life. But what should we really be telling Terry?

WILL GOD PROVIDE?

How should the church respond to individuals who struggle with same-sex attraction? We can begin by reflecting on a shared concern: God's provision. Many people today are asking whether God will provide. When we look at the shape of the economy, will God provide? When we consider the possibility of unemployment, will God provide? When we look at the health of our families, will God provide?

So how should the church support those in our midst with the enduring condition of same-sex attraction? Perhaps with the message that God will provide.

But I do not believe there's a formula for how God provides. This is perhaps one of the most difficult realities for most Christians to face. There's no algorithm that lets us figure out ahead of time how it will all work out. Rather, we see throughout Scripture and church history that God's provision doesn't always come in the way we want or expect. He provides to advance His purposes. We may try to read back into Scripture some preset formula, but that is the human tendency to do what humans do: we want to organize events and relationships, even our relationship with God, so that they make sense and are predictable.

So will God provide? Although I am focusing specifically on same-sex attraction, I want to recognize that the question is one we all ask, whether it is about our finances, our health, our family, our grades, our career, or our sexuality.

My invitation is to encourage the church to change the way it thinks about what matters most. Sometimes people in the church can get caught up in self-actualization, or, more specifically, sexual self-actualization, a common spirit of our culture. In other words, we tend to justify the things that we want rather than being obedient to what God wants for us. I want to shore up our faith within the church to be prepared to talk about stewardship of all we are, including our sexuality and sexual identity.

The question of whether or not God can provide almost automatically triggers the debate about the causes of homosexuality and whether it can change. Recall that I began and concluded chapter 3 with the same idea: We don't know. When it comes to a definitive statement about the cause of homosexuality, we don't know.

We often follow up that debate with the one on change. Recall that in chapter 4, I concluded that some people report meaningful change, but not all do. Also, many people only experience modest gains when they try to change their sexual orientation. Very few, if any, experience a 180-degree change from gay to straight. Yet the church often seems to expect this 180-degree change when a believer contends with same-sex attraction.

We are not the first people to get caught up in the cause and change debates. Remember Jesus' disciples?

> As he went along, he saw a man blind from birth. His disciples asked him, "Rabbi, who sinned, this man or his parents, that he was born blind?" [Jesus answered,] "Neither this man nor his parents sinned, but this happened so that the work of God might be displayed in his life" (John 9:1–3).

This passage is specifically about causes. The disciples wanted to know who sinned that caused the man's condition. But Jesus did not give them the answer they expected. Rather, He moved the discussion to the issue of God's higher purposes.

Who sinned—Linda or Linda's parents—that she has cancer?

Who sinned—Terry or Terry's parents—that he struggles with homosexuality?

None of them sinned. So how do we understand Terry's experience of same-sex attraction? Again, we do not know what causes homosexuality, but we don't need to know the answer to that to know how to respond to it. What we really need to answer is whether, regardless of our circumstances, God can provide. But keep in mind that we might end up surprised by what His provision looks like.

Purpose and Stewardship

I came across the specific applications of the John 9 passage when I was reading C. S. Lewis. I read this quote several years ago, not knowing that Lewis had ever written about homosexuality:

> I take it for certain that the *physical* satisfaction of homosexual desires is sin. This leaves the [homosexual] no worse off than any normal person who is, for whatever reason, prevented from marrying. . . . our speculations on the cause of the abnormality are not what matters and we must be content with ignorance. The disciples were not told *why* (in terms of efficient cause) the man was born blind (Jn. IX 1–3): only the final cause, that the works of God [should] be made manifest in him. This suggests that in homosexuality, as in every other tribulation, those works can be made manifest: i.e. that every disability conceals a vocation, if only we can find it. . . ."[1]

Change of sexual orientation has become a focus of both liberals and conservatives in the church today. Liberals bring it up to claim that God never intended for there to be only one orientation, so people don't need to change who they really are. Liberals have a stake in demonstrating and believing that people do not change.

Conservatives bring up reorientation by saying that God brings about change of orientation through healing or professional counseling. They have a stake in demonstrating and believing that people do change.

As I mentioned in chapter 2, I think a focus on sexual identity can be a helpful alternative to this focus on orientation. To begin, the gospel does not hinge on whether people can experience change of sexual orientation. It is interesting to me that C. S. Lewis doesn't entertain the option of change in the quote above. He seems to take homosexuality as a given, a reality, but he doesn't advise anyone to do anything specifically to experience change. Rather, he brings our focus to vocation. And sexual identity can be a resource to help people think vocationally. The idea of "vocation" has to do with one's purpose in life. It refers to who we are and what we intend to become. You see, sexual identity helps people focus on an end point; it can help us think about whose kingdom we are a part of. Is our identity to be found in our sexual attractions or in Christ?

God may choose to bring about healing this side of eternity, but He often chooses not to. Indeed, a few years ago I met a man who spoke of his direct and miraculous healing from his sexual attractions. He had an amazing testimony, and I did not doubt his experience of healing. But as we spoke about his life and healing, even he shared with me that his experience is not typical. He indicated that most people do not experience a miraculous healing but will continue to contend with their attractions, often for the rest of their lives.

Why? We can point to the fall and to the ways in which we may all contend with events and circumstances that are not what God originally intended for us. But there can also be a larger purpose, a transcendent purpose that we often overlook.

As we read about in John 9, God's purpose is to bring glory to His name, to make us holy, to set us apart for His purposes.

This is a question of stewardship. In the church today, can we be stewards of our sexuality? What does that mean?

As we mentioned in the previous chapter, it is important to keep in mind that any talk of stewardship flies in the face of our culture. To talk this way means swimming upstream against the current. The current is moving one way in our culture—toward self-actualization; that is, realizing our potential by tuning in to our impulses and following them as reliable guides to what is ultimately meaningful and personally fulfilling.

This contrasts sharply with a Christian understanding of the human condition and the trustworthiness of our impulses. As C. S. Lewis noted in *The Abolition of Man*:

> But why ought we to obey instincts? Is there another instinct of a higher order directing us to do so, and a third of a still higher order directing us to obey *it?*—an infinite regress of instincts? This is presumably impossible, but nothing else will serve. From the statement of psychological fact "I have an impulse to do so and so" we cannot by any ingenuity derive the practical principle "I ought to obey this impulse." . . .
>
> Telling us to obey instinct is like telling us to obey "people." People say different things: so do instincts. Our instincts are at war.[2]

Christianity rejects the idea that our impulses are reliable moral guides. The Christian has to look outside of him or herself for direction on how to live.

Stewardship, then, involves recognizing that we are not the owners of our sexuality but rather that we steward our sexuality, just as we steward the rest of who we are and what we have been given.

The language of stewardship is important, but it might be hard to grasp at first. We are raised in our culture to think of ownership. We define ourselves by our accomplishments and our possessions, by what we have attained and by what we own. We think of our homes as ours. We think of our jobs as ours. We think of our children as ours. We think of our cars as ours. In fact, we think of the lane we are driving our cars in as ours! I recently read the bestselling book *Traffic: Why We Drive the Way We Do (and What It Says About Us)* by Tom Vanderbilt. It is an interesting book about so many aspects of driving and traffic patterns and congestion (often caused by gawkers) and all the different kinds of professionals paid to deal with traffic concerns. In any case, he shared some of the research that's been conducted on people's perceptions when driving, and how it is that we project ourselves beyond our cars and into the lane we are in. In other words, we think of the lane we are in as being an extension of ourselves. We can actually get angry when someone way ahead of us moves into *our lane*. We move quickly and effortlessly from *ourselves* to *our* car to *our* lane through this projection. If we struggle with lanes on public highways, is it any wonder why the concept of stewardship would seem odd when applied to an individual's sexuality?

But it is not the concept of stewardship that is the issue. Rather, it is a culture in which we focus on what we have, what we own, and what is ours. The language of stewardship is not incorrect, but the fact that it sounds foreign to our ears should be reason to give us pause. We are far too shaped by our culture, and significant changes would have to take place to equip or prepare us to think about ourselves and our sexuality in truly Christian terms.

To steward our sexuality is to look outside ourselves and our experiences toward a trustworthy guide. We need to look to Scripture and the work of the Spirit in order to understand our thoughts, impulses, and experiences so that we can live in conformity to God's revealed will for sexuality and its expression.

How accessible is the concept of stewardship to the average Christian? Do Paul's words to the church in Corinth even resonate with contemporary Christians? "You are not your own; you were bought at a price. Therefore honor God with your body" (1 Corinthians 6:19). My experience has been that mature Christians recognize the importance of stewardship in all areas of their lives and are not surprised to see stewardship extend to their sexuality. They steward their time, their resources, their finances, and so on. They don't act as if it is theirs. Rather, they see all of what they have and all of who they are as something to steward.

But this is not a concept that is taught and lived out consistently in most Christian communities. That is undoubtedly a result, at least in part, of living in a society that prizes personal possessions and actualizing our individual potential. Because we as the church struggle to instill the meaning and experience of sanctification into the lives of young people and perhaps fail to live it consistently in our own lives, is it any wonder that Christians who experience same-sex attraction find the current version of the gay script discussed in chapter 2 so compelling?

PRINCIPLES TO PRACTICE IN RELATIONSHIPS

Not everyone will agree that they are to steward their sexuality. It may be helpful to return to the distinction we made in chapter 7 between the assertive advocate and the sincere struggler when we think about those we know and interact with.

The Assertive Advocate

Rather than talk about all assertive advocates, I want to talk specifically about the assertive advocate who is a part of the church. They love the church but want to see it change its central teachings on sexuality and sexual behavior. They reject the language of *love the sinner but hate the sin*. They would argue that it is a false dichotomy, that *loving who I am means loving what I do, as what I do is an extension of who I am.*

Does this remind you of anything? It reflects the gay script we discussed in chapter 2. Remember that the gay script collapses attraction, orientation, and identity into one thing, treating attractions as synonymous with identity. They firmly believe that the love you show them must express itself by your agreeing that homosexuality reflects God's diverse plan for creation, and that same-sex behavior is an expression of identity and diversity rather than a moral concern.

The assertive advocate is coming from a position in which the gay script is a central, organizing way of understanding his or her experiences. So how should we interact with the assertive advocate?

Lead by example. I was recently reading *Signature Sins* by Michael Mangis, a truly insightful book that deals with the premise that we all have our own primary areas in which we struggle. These signature sins vary from person to person. While we all share a common plight as sinners living in a fallen world, we all experience our struggle with a unique cluster of sins in our own way.

I know that the things I struggle with in my own Christian walk, sins such as envy or pride, do not cause me to receive the same kind of scrutiny as the person who struggles with same-sex attraction. In other words, we must be careful not to ask those who experience same-sex attraction to steward their sexuality if the rest of us do not steward the different parts of our lives we struggle with, including, for some, our own sexuality. For example, do you actively promote abstinence until marriage, or do you believe premarital sex is the norm? What about pornography?

My experience is that those who struggle with homosexuality are quite aware of and sensitive to hypocrisy in the church. They know when they are being asked to do something that others are not. If you agree that sexual minorities could benefit from following a curriculum of Christlikeness, then follow that curriculum in your own life. It is always better to lead by example, which will give you credibility to speak to the benefits of following such a curriculum. Put differently, if you believe in stewarding your sexuality, then lead by example, living out the principles you promote.

Practice "convicted civility." Richard Mouw, the president of Fuller Theological Seminary, came up with this helpful phrase. He was trying to balance the idea that Christians should hold on to their beliefs and values (in other words, their "convictions") while engaging others in ways that convey mutual respect and a high regard for those with whom they disagree. Putting these together, Mouw calls for "convicted civility."

My experience is that most Christians struggle with how to hold these two dimensions together. For some Christians, conviction is easier; they know what they believe about homosexuality and they lead with that, often missing out on constructive and meaningful engagement with others. For other Christians, civility is most important; they focus so much on being in relationship that they fail to see how their faith matters in the discussion. Their beliefs and values can be difficult to articulate when facing potential disagreements.

With the assertive advocate, it will be important to hold both conviction and civility in balance.

Listen and share. It is important to listen to the assertive advocate. It is important to listen to anyone, of course, but the assertive advocate expects that you won't listen. Of course, they might define "listening" as agreeing with them, so you may have to clarify that.

You can follow the same advice as you share with them your own understanding. You should not assume that they have to agree with you to show that they are listening.

You can listen and reflect on the different weights a person gives to various aspects of their sexual identity. One person may give greater weight to their biological sex, religious values, etc., while another person may give greater weight to their attractions to the same sex.

Encourage them in their walk with God. There can be times when it is tempting to steer clear of assertive advocates, to only hang out with people with whom you already agree. But keep in mind that even if there appears to be a number of differences between you and the assertive advocate, the one thing you hold in common is a relationship with God. Encourage them in that walk—not so that they will change their view on this topic or any other topic, but because it is good for all of us to grow in our relationship with God and to allow Him to speak to us and work in our lives to further His purposes.

The Sincere Struggler

So how should the church be communicating with and encouraging the sincere strugglers in their walk with the Lord? There are three things that I think we can keep in mind.

Solid foundation. The sincere strugglers I have known who have been able to move forward in a practical understanding of stewardship had a solid foundation in the Word of God. Whenever I think of establishing a solid foundation, I am reminded of Gary Thomas's book on marriage. It is titled *Sacred Marriage,* and the subtitle is, *What If God Intended Marriage to Make Us Holy Rather Than Happy?*

Gary makes a convincing case that a Christian view of marriage contrasts sharply with that of the world. It's not that Christians don't believe that marriage can make us happy, or that happiness is a bad thing. But Christians are not to embrace a secular view of marriage— that is, that the purpose of marriage is to make us happy. That isn't a Christian view at all. Rather, God intends for marriage to be a relationship that He uses to make us more Christlike, to make us holy.

A similar question can be asked of our sexual identity—what if God's intention is to make us holy rather than happy? It's not that God is against our happiness, but God may be asking us to pursue Him first and to find our fulfillment and happiness in Him rather than in what the world offers.

> What is more, I consider everything a loss compared to the surpassing greatness of knowing Christ Jesus my Lord, for whose sake I have lost all things. I consider them rubbish, that I may gain Christ…. I want to know Christ and the power of his resurrection and the fellowship of sharing in his sufferings, becoming like him in His death, and so, somehow, to attain to the resurrection of the dead. (Philippians 3:8, 10–11)

Proper perspective. Remember you are Christ's own. My children are getting older now, but for years the only movies my wife and I saw were animated, so that is where I get most of my movie illustrations from. If you've seen *The Lion King*, you will remember the scene in which Simba has grown up away from home and in shame. Simba had been led to believe he killed his father until Rafiki, an ornery monkey, comes along, hits him on the head with a stick, and proclaims that he's seen Simba's dad. A chase ensues in which Simba follows Rafiki through the dense foliage and up to a body of water. The monkey points to the reflection of Simba in the water. We then hear the booming voice of none other than James Earl Jones saying, "Remember who you are." You see, Simba had forgotten who he was. He had forgotten he was the heir to the throne. He had forgotten his identity.

Remember who you are. It's a matter of identity. The sincere strugglers I have known who have been able to move forward in stewarding their sexuality kept their lives in proper perspective. They knew who they were. They knew *whose* they were. Their identity was formed around the person of Jesus. Their identity was *in Christ*.

It is in this context that I might encourage the sincere struggler to describe experiences rather than identify with them. Think about the three-tier distinction between attractions, orientation, and identity. Stay descriptive while respecting a person's right to make decisions about identity and behavior.

It may also be helpful to reflect on the different scripts from which we read. Do these scripts collapse the three-tier distinction we introduced in chapter 2 between same-sex attractions, a homosexual orientation, and a gay identity? Do they presume the discovery metaphor—that individuals should recognize their same-sex attractions as an indication of who they really are, which is a categorically different type of person from most others? Using more descriptive language encourages us to talk about decisions people make about whether or not to integrate experiences of same-sex attraction into a gay identity. Perhaps same-sex attractions signal not a categorical distinction among types of persons, but rather one of many reflections of the fall.

Perseverance. The last point I want to make to the sincere struggler is that the path they are on requires perseverance. I remember meeting with a young woman, Jean, several years ago. In the first year of our work she had trouble even acknowledging to herself that she was struggling with same-sex attraction. She had recently left a same-sex relationship, but she thought of it as a one-time thing rather than an ongoing struggle; it was an attraction to a specific woman, but in her mind (and in her experience up to that time), it did not mean she was really attracted to the same sex. Jean experienced several turning points in regard to how she understood her situation, but one was when she began to explore her attractions and her susceptibility to the kind of relationship she had just left—a relationship that had been harmful to her.

But the other major turning point came when she visited a church and was invited by a woman to join her and other women for a Bible study. Jean was anxious about it, but she decided to give it a try. Over the course of the next year, she shared with the women in the group and they shared with her. She was not ready at this time to share the specific nature of her struggle (with same-sex attraction), but she was able to talk about a failed relationship, the grief she felt, and other challenges that come from losing someone you are close to. She grew tremendously in her faith that year, and she delighted in the fellowship with other women who took their faith seriously.

A year or so after that Bible study was completed, Jean ended up joining a ministry that focused more specifically on sexuality. She was finally ready to explore these concerns more directly with others who faced similar challenges.

Many people make the mistake of jumping in too deep too soon. There is something to be said for staying the course. This requires realistic expectations and patience.

I was reminded again of the idea of perseverance when I faced some challenges a few years ago. A family member sent me a letter that was a great encouragement to me.

What does it mean to *test* faith? Trials (troubles) test our faith. Why? Because they cause us to question God's promises. They undermine our confident assurance that those things we've not yet seen are going to happen. We've not yet seen them, and this awful thing that's happening to me now makes me wonder if I ever *will* see them.

Yet it is at *this* point that endurance comes into the picture—what is endurance? What is its relationship to faith? If we no longer have confident assurance about things we cannot see, if we are haunted by doubt, or if we are simply so weary or in so much anguish that the things we cannot see become *unreal* to us, it is endurance that makes us continue on, no matter what. It is, in a sense, a willfully blind obedience to God, a stubborn determination to go on, almost like Jacob wrestling with God and refusing to let go until God blessed him.

It is somewhat difficult to reconcile this with James' admonition to consider trials an opportunity for joy—not *because* of the trial, per se, but because of the opportunity to endure. This is an *opportunity* because it *results* in strong character—in a Christian who is ready for anything. . . .

All of this would seem to imply that a Christian whose faith is never tested would not be much of a Christian at all! In other words, God builds into the Christian life aspects of character development that would *not* be possible (I think) outside of a fallen world. Here we *must* face situations in which we are *genuinely* tempted to throw in the towel, so that we can also have the *genuine* opportunity to press on, and in pressing on we gain a victory (even a small victory) of faith, and in doing that we develop our own Christian history, our personal Christian memory, which is an integral part of our individual character. We can see what we've been through and how God brought us through it, and we are ready to face whatever happens next, not because of ourselves, but because of what God already has done for us and in us.

If the sincere struggler is attempting to change their orientation, I would support them in their attempt. The difference in what I recommend and what I see happening is that today most people who attempt change do so in isolation and in shame, with high expectations that they become completely heterosexual. I recommend *realistic, modest expectations*. For example, Christians often turn to 1 Corinthians 6:11 to talk about expectations of complete and categorical change in sexual orientation. After all, isn't Paul saying that some of the people in Corinth were homosexual at one time and are now heterosexual? I don't think we can draw this conclusion from the text. What I think we can say with greater confidence is that people had engaged in patterns of behavior that fell outside of God's revealed will. Perhaps the pattern of behavior also reflected in some way a condition of the heart. But with the change in behavior came a change in identity, a change in heart. You were this type of a person (a person who engaged in this pattern of behavior), but now you are not. This is similar to what Paul is saying about those who committed adultery. *Such were some of you. Some of you were adulterers.*[3] People ceased to be adulterers when they ceased a pattern of behavior (sex with someone other than their spouse) that characterized them and reflected a condition of their heart.

That isn't to say that the only thing a person can expect is to change behavior, as important as that is. I would certainly support people in their change attempt. Perhaps people you know are active in an Exodus-affiliated ministry or are meeting with a counselor about change. If they are attempting change, they are doing something that takes time and that has an emotional cost, and there is a need to come alongside them in that.

At the same time, I want us to keep in mind that love for those who attempt complete change is not contingent on their outcome. Nor is their spiritual maturity contingent on a categorical change from gay to straight. They may make real and meaningful gains, but they should not feel from their friends the added pressure to be free from all struggles in this area. Also, keep in mind that as they navigate this difficult terrain, they are learning important life lessons that can be helpful to you and (eventually) to others. They have a lot to offer you and the broader Christian community through the steps they are taking by saying no to one thing in order to say yes to another.

It is also in this context that I want to help them avoid isolation or diminished social support. Will you be there for them throughout their change attempt and beyond, regardless of the degree of success?

Perseverance is aided by having others who share a person's beliefs and values. It is difficult enough to persevere, but to do so by oneself is tragic when there is a Christian community that could provide support. Social support in this case needs to be an encouraging, empathetic presence—sustained over time—from someone who genuinely understands what the person is doing and at what cost.

A Lesson in Grammar and Punctuation

Have you read a good book on grammar lately? I know, it's a strange question. Several years ago I read *Eats, Shoots & Leaves* by Lynne Truss. It's a funny and engaging book on grammar and punctuation. In it she shares this story:

> A panda walks into a café. He orders a sandwich, eats it, then draws a gun and fires two shots in the air.
>
> "Why?" asks the confused waiter, as the panda makes toward the exit. The panda produces a badly punctuated wildlife manual and tosses it over his shoulder.
>
> "I'm a panda," he says, at the door. "Look it up."
>
> The waiter turns to the relevant entry and, sure enough, finds an explanation.
>
> "Panda. Large black-and-white bear-like mammal, native to China. Eats, shoots and leaves."[4]

Lynne Truss's conclusion: "So, punctuation really does matter, even if it is only occasionally a matter of life and death."[5]

When we look at sexual identity, we should explore the words we use and the stress we place on certain concepts—in other words, how we "punctuate" such questions as what causes same-sex feelings and whether they can be changed. We can learn how our words and "punctuation" can help and hinder our ability to be extensions of God's redemptive work in the lives of others.

We would do well to identify and edit the scripts from which people read today, and we can begin with punctuation.[6] The person who experiences same-sex attraction can only see the period. No commas, no parentheses, no exclamation points. Just the period. They assume their perspective is the only one. They don't think there is any room for alternative responses. The British refer to these as "full stops," and you can see why.

> "I experience same-sex attraction." Period.
> "Experiences of same-sex attraction signal who I really am." Period.
> "I'm gay." Period.
> "The church can't deal with me. The church can't care for me." Period.

Compare this to what Jesus says as He offers so much more than the struggler expects:

> "Cast your cares on [me] and [I] will sustain you!" (Psalm 55:22). Exclamation point.
> You say: "I'm afraid." Period.
> But Jesus says: "Do not be not afraid, for I am with you!" (Genesis 26:24). Exclamation point.
> You say: "But you don't understand my circumstances." Period. "What do you know of my struggle?"
> Jesus says: "[I] work for the good of those who love [me]!" (Romans 8:28). Exclamation point.
> You ask: "Aren't I alone?"
> But Jesus says: "[I] will never leave you nor forsake you!" (Deuteronomy 31:6). Exclamation point.

What we see here is a shift in approach. Once the end is no longer a foregone conclusion, the struggling individual can move from "How do I make sense of my faith in light of my sexual identity?" to

"How do I make sense of my sexual identity in light of my faith in God's goodness?"

We all have a tendency to do this, to put periods on our lives, as if the end of the road for us were a foregone conclusion. It's hopeless. It's over. It's finished.

Whether or not this is your struggle (homosexuality), you can begin to ask yourself about punctuation in your own life. It is a question of making meaning out of our circumstances, including those situations and besetting conditions that cause us distress.

So we would do well to help each other with punctuation. We can do this by listening for the "periods" or "full stops." If you are the friend of someone who is sorting out sexual identity questions, come alongside those who are particularly prone to "full stops."

Be Patient and Respect the Process

It would be nice to be able to provide quick answers for those who are struggling with same-sex attraction, but of course it's never that easy. As you come alongside struggling individuals, be careful not to force exclamation points on them. Respect the process. It is usually a slow change from periods to exclamation points. Notice from the dialogue above that often exclamation points are preceded by a question mark. It may take years, but in time all periods are transformed—by God's grace—into exclamation points.

Years ago when my wife and I were starting our family, we came to find out that we were unable to have biological children. We struggled with infertility. We struggled with many questions about God's plan for us and His provision. We wondered what went wrong. Why us? was a question that was hard to answer.

Many well-meaning Christians offered us their "support." They either gave us theological pearls of wisdom ("All things are possible with God!" or "All things work together for good!" or "God will provide!") or suggested home remedies ("Wear boxer shorts!").

It's not that they said things we disagreed with theologically. We believed God could provide; we knew that intellectually. But we were suffering. We were struggling with doubts and we didn't seem to be experiencing God. I felt that many of their attempts to provide support were really about assuring themselves that everything was fine. They were unwilling to step into our pain, to sit with us in our questions and doubts.

For us, we found great healing in a small group of fellow Christians, some of whom had struggled to varying degrees with infertility. There was instant credibility there. We could listen to them. We could hear what they had to say, because their words were seasoned with life experiences. But do you know what? They didn't tend to say as much as those who offered platitudes. No, the small group we were a part of just listened. They created a space for us to share our experience, and they sat with us—letting us be where we were.

So when we think of homosexuality more as an enduring condition, we would do well to learn to sit with others in their experience, to sit with them in their questions.

When we think of grammar and punctuation, we can think of how all of us in the community of faith are to relate to God as the author, and to the Holy Spirit as the one who guides us in the editing.

So with that understanding in mind, we can patiently support those who are trying to figure out which way to approach their besetting condition. Do they say, "I am gay, and I'm sorting out what to do with my Christianity"? Or do they go a different direction: "I am a Christian, and I am sorting out what to do with the fact that I experience same-sex attraction"?

TAKE-HOME POINTS

- Although some people who attempt change of orientation may experience meaningful change, most will experience modest gains, often acknowledging that they still experience some same-sex attractions.

- The church often responds constructively to other enduring conditions, but it has struggled to come alongside those with same-sex attractions.

- God's provision may take different, often unexpected, forms.

- Listen for the "periods" people place on their own lives.

- Avoid forcing "exclamation points" on the lives of others.

- Come alongside those who are sorting out these issues and trying to live faithfully before God.

CHAPTER TEN

Concluding Thoughts

The topics of homosexuality and sexual identity are difficult ones for Christians. There is pressure placed on believers from a number of directions, and it is not easy to know how best to understand the many issues that come up. With that in mind, it may be helpful to go back over what we've learned, filling in a few holes here and there, and introducing some concluding thoughts. So in this chapter I will briefly summarize what we've learned by reminding you of the different people we've met along the way and the challenges that each faced.

WHAT DOES GOD THINK ABOUT HOMOSEXUALITY?

We began with a look at the question, What does God think about homosexuality? I introduced you to Scott, a teen whose parents dropped him off for counseling. Scott had a genuine faith and wanted an honest answer to this difficult question.

We acknowledged that we must approach any questions about "What God thinks . . ." with humility, while acknowledging that the

Bible is a reliable source of information and guidance in all matters of faith and life, including sexuality and sexual behavior.

If I were talking to a young person about this question, I would say that, rather than focusing on a handful of passages, I think it makes more sense to look at the overall biblical witness regarding sexuality. This can be done by looking at (a) God's intentions as He created us for monogamous, heterosexual unions; (b) the impact of the fall on all of human experience, including our sexuality; (c) God's plan of redemption and the role that marriage plays in being a providential structure for sexual behavior; and (d) glorification, which reminds us that our primary identity is as part of the body of Christ, the church.

I recognize, too, that Scripture is the Christian's primary source of authority, but there are others as well. For Scott, what the Bible says about homosexuality played an important role in the decisions he made. At the same time, Christians can acknowledge that there are other sources of information available to the believer who is trying to address the question of "What God thinks" about a topic. These include Christian tradition, reason, and experience.

We looked at how Christian tradition, which is largely based on previous believers' understanding of the Bible, is supportive of the view that God's intention is for sex to occur in marriage between a man and woman who have made a commitment to be faithful to one another for a lifetime. Departures from this position are quite radical, though they have been forcefully advanced in the past thirty years and have taken on a quality that places great pressure on conservatives who still hold to the Christian sexual ethic.

We also looked at how our culture typically uses the term *reason* to refer to scientific findings about sexual orientation. While research attempting to answer questions about how common homosexuality is, the causes of homosexuality, mental health concerns associated with homosexuality, and the possibility of change of orientation are interesting, they do not settle the moral debate for the church. The moral debate is primarily a theological concern, which will only be settled by an accurate understanding of Scripture rather than descriptive findings from science. The theological issues can be informed, but not decided, by good scientific studies.

The fourth source of information or authority in response to the question "What does God think about homosexuality?" is personal experience. In these discussions, personal experience often refers to listening to those Christians who wish to change the church's moral teaching in matters of sexuality—in other words, those who want the church to make room for same-sex relationships. While it is true that the church should listen to the experiences of believers who identify as gay, we need to keep in mind that they are not the only voices to be heard in this discussion. The church should also listen to the experiences of believers who have chosen not to form a gay identity and who instead are saying no to that aspect of themselves so they can say yes to what they believe God calls them to.

This was helpful to Scott as he thought through these issues. Not only was he able to study Scripture and reflect on Christian tradition, but he was also able to look at how science related to the question he was asking, and to identify people who, like him, were wondering about this question and trying to make a decision that was in keeping with God's revealed will. When I last saw Scott, he did not want to follow his parents' request to change orientation, nor did he want to adopt a gay identity. He did not identify with a gay identity or the people or organizations that would support it. Rather, he simply wanted the time and space to explore questions he had about a Christian understanding of sexuality and sexual identity so that he could feel peace about God's will for his life in this area.

At the end of this first chapter, I pointed out that all believers are encouraged to reflect on the relative weight they give to these different sources of information or authority. Everyone with an opinion on the matter should be able to identify which source or sources of authority are trump for them in these discussions: the Bible, Christian tradition, reason, or personal experience. Everyone favors one or two sources of authority over the others.

WHY IS SEXUAL IDENTITY THE HEART OF THE MATTER?

Much of this chapter introduced the concept of sexual identity. I did this by making a distinction between same-sex attraction, a homosexual orientation, and a gay identity. To talk about same-sex attraction is to use the most descriptive language possible, since when we say a person is "same-sex attracted," we are merely describing their physical and emotional attraction toward the same sex. Using the term "homosexual orientation" is also descriptive, but it acknowledges that the person's attractions toward the same sex are significant, and that they persist over time. To talk about a gay identity is to enter into language that is part of a modern sociocultural movement. It is to join others who, for the first time in history, use the self-identifying label "I am gay" to attribute who they are to their experience of same-sex attraction. It is a way of defining oneself by a single attribute, and then adopting a set of attitudes and behaviors that correspond with how our culture defines "gay."

There is a kind of developmental path toward forming a gay identity that typically involves three broad stages: identity *dilemma*, identity *development*, and identity *synthesis*. Our understanding today is that sexual identity development begins with sexual attraction starting around age ten or twelve, and may involve same-sex behaviors around the ages of thirteen to fourteen for those who engage in same-sex behavior. Same-sex behavior may be followed by a questioning of identity and then, for some, labeling of themselves as gay at around age fifteen.

It was in this chapter that I asked you to imagine a sixteen-year-old named Chris. Like so many other adolescents who experience same-sex attraction, Chris is looking for help in figuring out who he is and what his experiences are all about. I asked you to imagine that Chris is like an actor on a stage. Like any actor, Chris is looking for a script that will help him understand his character and show him how to relate to others; he is looking for a script that will inform him about his identity.

I suggested that recent research on those who experience same-sex attraction but do not integrate their sexual attractions into a gay identity suggests that there is a difference between what I referred to as a "gay script" and alternative scripts. The gay script looks like this:

- Same-sex attractions signal a naturally-occurring or "intended by God" distinction between homosexuality, heterosexuality, and bisexuality.

- Same-sex attractions signal who you really are as a person (emphasis on *discovery*).

- Same-sex attractions are at the core of who you are as a person.

- Same-sex behavior is an extension of that core.

- Self-actualization (behaviors that match who you really are) of your sexual identity is crucial for your fulfillment.

The gay script relies heavily on the discovery metaphor by emphasizing the fact that same-sex attractions signal who a person really is. By doing this, the script categorizes people based on their sexual attractions. In other words, people are defined by who they are attracted to and do not have any choices in the matter.

Alternative scripts focus on the metaphor of "integration" and emphasize the fact that people can choose their identities, regardless of their same-sex attractions. One such alternative is an "identity in Christ" script. Here are that script's basic points:

- Same-sex attraction signals *not* a categorical distinction among types of persons, but one of many human experiences that are "not the way things are supposed to be."

- Same-sex attractions are part of your experience, but not the defining element of your identity.

- You can choose to integrate your experiences of attraction to the same sex into a gay identity.

- On the other hand, you can instead choose to center your

identity around other aspects of your experience, including your biological sex, gender identity, and so on.

• The most compelling aspect of personhood for the Christian is one's identity *in Christ*, a central and defining aspect of what it means to be a follower of Jesus.

As we mentioned above, rather than relying on the discovery metaphor, this script relies on the metaphor of integration. Integration is about taking various parts and making them into a unified whole. The integration metaphor sees same-sex attraction as only one part of an individual, not the sole defining feature. It then recognizes that a young person has choices to make about both behavior and identity. A young person can integrate his or her attractions into a gay identity or they can form their identity around something else. There are a variety of options at this point.

One thing we should keep in mind is that being gay can mean different things to different people. Some Christians call themselves gay when they simply mean that they have same-sex attractions. I mentioned how this was true for a young man named Rob. Rob saw himself as being honest with others about what he experiences. People like Rob may believe in the traditional Christian sexual ethic and lead chaste lives, but they use the designation "gay" to convey something about their sexual attraction. When I last saw Rob he seemed at peace with his decisions about identity and his efforts to maintain chastity. The challenge he faced was finding ways to relate to his family; they did not understand "gay as synonymous with same-sex attractions" as a starting point and felt he should experience a greater change in attractions or orientation. This points to one of the challenges faced by those who adopt the more common identity label, as it currently carries with it meanings and connotations that many Christians will have a difficult time setting aside.

In any case, the experience of Rob and others like him is different from the person who, by saying they are gay and Christian, is saying that Christianity has been wrong about homosexuality and the traditional Christian sexual ethic. These individuals are typically advo-cating for a change in the church's understanding of sexual behavior, seeing homosexuality as simply another expression of God's diversity in the created order.

In any case, a discussion of sexual identity may lead to a more helpful and constructive dialogue than a narrow discussion of sexual orientation and whether or not it can change.

WHAT CAUSES HOMOSEXUALITY?

In this chapter I introduced you to Rick and his mother. Rick was a sixteen-year-old teen who recently admitted to his parents that he was gay. His mother struggled with this admission, partly because he had dated girls, so this gay identity just didn't seem to "fit" with what she knew about him. Like many parents, Rick's mom began to challenge him and his identity. She was searching for answers, asking questions like, What causes homosexuality?

I shared with her that people do not choose to experience same-sex attraction; it is something they find themselves experiencing. It is unclear how a person like Rick becomes attracted to the same sex. There is a lot we do not know at this time. But even though we don't have clear answers, people and organizations on both sides of the debate keep advancing their positions. One side believes nature is the main cause; the other side believes nurture is to blame.

As far as the nature side of the argument is concerned, although researchers have been working hard on the biological hypothesis in the past twenty years, the results are mixed. But on the nurture side, the research on environmental causes of homosexuality is also mixed.

There is a tendency in the debates about the causes of homo-sexuality to commit the error of "nothing-but-ism." In other words, people tend to claim that the cause of homosexuality is "nothing but _____," with people inserting their preferred causes, either derived from nature or nurture. The church is inclined to commit this error in the direction of two theories in particular: parent-child relationships and childhood sexual abuse. Granted, the work in this area has been largely ignored in favor of advancing the biological hypothesis, but the studies that have been conducted are not that compelling. While environment appears to play some role for some people, it is unclear what that role is.

When Rick's mom began to search for answers and ask if there was something she and her husband did (or did not do) to cause Rick's homosexuality, I shared with them that I didn't think so. At this time, there does not appear to be any one cause of same-sex attraction or a homosexual orientation. There appear to be many factors that may contribute to same-sex attraction or a homosexual orientation, and these factors are probably weighted differently for different people.

When I last met with Rick and his mother, they both expressed appreciation for giving them their sense of family once again. They looked at Rick's same-sex attractions differently: Rick saw his attractions as signaling his identity, while his mother viewed his attractions as a reflection of the fall. But she had found ways to respectfully communicate her concerns to Rick while recognizing as he turned eighteen that he had his own choices to make about his life, behavior, and identity. She took the long view, recognizing that Rick may be sorting out sexual identity issues for years to come, and she positioned herself to be a resource to him for the long haul.

I concluded this chapter by saying that the topic of what causes homosexuality is an area we should approach with humility. It is okay for the time being to be an *etiology* (causes) *agnostic* (don't know). A humble approach here may be helpful as we interact with the people we know and love who are sorting out what to do about their experiences of same-sex attraction.

CAN SOMEONE CHANGE SEXUAL ORIENTATION?

This chapter opened by introducing you to Shawn. Shawn's story is interesting because he had tried and tried and tried to change his sexual orientation before I met him. He had been in a thirty-week curriculum three times over the past three years, and he was wondering if he was doing enough. Although he had gained a tremendous amount of information and insight into his concerns, and although he felt he was growing spiritually and was appreciative of the social support he received, he was not experiencing a change in his sexual orientation.

The question of whether homosexuality can change is perhaps the most politically divisive question that can be asked in the fields of counseling or psychology. It is also a common question asked by many families dealing with sexual identity concerns. The research that has been conducted is far from ideal, and there is a need to further our understanding of what people can expect if they attempt to change their sexual orientation.

However, based on the research that is available at this time, it appears as though some people do experience a change in sexual attraction, although most experience modest gains, and many share that they continue to have same-sex attractions at times. This would suggest that a realistic expectation would not be categorical change (from completely gay to completely straight), but rather modest shifts along a continuum of attraction. What I mean by this is that there is likely to be some reduction in attraction to the same sex, which for some people makes chastity an easier option than it was before. On the other hand, a few people may experience some increase in attraction to the opposite sex (or to a specific person, such as a spouse). Some report that this is heterosexuality, although they often also acknowledge some remaining attraction to the same sex.

The question of whether attempting to change sexual orientation is harmful has also been raised. It is unclear if the "harm" occurs when just talking about the change attempt, or as the particular methods are used, or because of the strict expectations that were placed before them (a 180-degree change from gay to straight). In other words, some people have been hurt, but it is hard to say what caused that. Their pain could be due to unrealistic expectations, poor or misguided or incompetent guidance in this area, or some other cause that is unclear at this time.

Recent research suggests that it does not appear to be intrinsically harmful to try to change sexual orientation, especially if a person has realistic expectations. I think Shawn is a good example of someone who was not harmed in his attempt to change, even though he worked at it for three years. However, the biggest struggle is usually with unrealistic expectations or with messages that the individual is not trying hard enough or does not have enough faith. When I met Shawn he was still wondering if he had tried hard enough. There may be a point at which we want to explore other options for someone like Shawn, so that they can receive the benefits of social support and faith-based resources for growing in spiritual maturity, even if they do not experience a significant change in sexual attractions or orientation.

Shawn continues to experience same-sex attraction. He is no longer actively pursuing change of sexual orientation, but he continues to explore his identity in light of ongoing attraction to the same sex. He identifies himself as a Christian and is honest about his same-sex attractions; however, he does not identify as gay. He is involved in a local church community and is building a social support network that can be a resource to him now and in the years to come.

WHAT IF MY CHILD OR TEEN ANNOUNCES A GAY IDENTITY?

In part 2 of the book, "Honest Answers to Questions Facing Families," we tackled the first question, "What if my child or teen announces a gay identity?" I introduced you to an anxious mother whose young son, Jeremy, was doing "girlish things" that were causing her anxiety. In her mind, Jeremy seemed to be identifying more with her than with her husband, and she asked the question that some parents ask under these circumstances: Is my child gay?

This chapter tackled two questions. The first was, How do we know if a child is likely to experience same-sex attraction? That is what Jeremy's mother was asking. The second question was, How do parents respond to a teen who is identifying as gay?

Throughout this chapter I reminded parents that there is no one cause of homosexuality, including their relationship with their child. I want to provide parents with some emotional space so that they are not overwhelmed by the tendency to blame themselves when an issue like this arises.

What we do know is that "gender nonconformity" (boys acting like girls or girls acting like boys) is probably the most consistent experience adults with a homosexual orientation report from their childhood. But most kids who are outside of the box of social expectations (of being a boy or a girl) do not grow up to identify as gay or lesbian.

Although we do not know at this time what causes homosexuality, most experts agree that some combination of both nature and nurture plays a role. Because the environment (and how a young person responds to their environment) appears to play a part, it may make sense for parents to take some of the steps that have been helpful in resolving gender identity questions. But many people see these not as interventions so much as simply clear and consistent messages about gender. The goal is to genuinely affirm a child in his or her interests while ignoring interests that don't match the child's gender, or sometimes gently redirecting the child toward interests that are more in keeping with traditional roles.

The second question we addressed in this chapter had to do with a teenager's sexual identity. The question was, How do parents respond to a teen who is identifying as gay? I introduced you to a mother who came in with her son, Phil, a seventeen-year-old who had recently admitted to being gay after his mother was informed of some suggestive photos of Phil on a social network site. As I mentioned in the chapter, by the time Phil's parents knew about his identity, he had already revealed it to many of his friends, who were quite supportive.

In this chapter I encouraged parents to stay calm and listen if their teen discloses same-sex attraction. Parents would do well to keep in mind the obstacles that get in the way of listening. These include strong emotional reactions, such as confusion, anger, or disappointment, but also reactions like guilt or shame, which are often tied to the idea that they as parents caused the homosexuality or that there is a kind of family shame associated with this particular issue in evangelical Christian homes.

When parents first hear about their teen's gay or lesbian identity, they tend to forget the developmental stage their adolescent is in, as he or she tries to form an identity, trying on various roles in different settings. Also, when it comes to homosexuality, teens are receiving a script that is compelling to them. The church has not offered an alternative script, one that prepares young people to understand their sexuality and what it means to live in Christ.

It is also important to remember that, in most instances, teens have been aware of their attractions long before parents have been made aware. Parents should give themselves time to process this information.

It is also essential for parents to attend to their marriage and not to underestimate the strain they are experiencing through this tumultuous time. Couples tend to become polarized in response to the strong emotions that come up as a result of the disclosure of a gay identity. These polarizing feelings typically fall into the *angry/confused* category on the one hand and the *loving/protective* category on the other. Usually both parents feel all of these emotions, but they can quickly become a caricature of either the anger or the protection side of the divide. It can be helpful to watch out for this and keep working through the full range of emotional reactions each parent feels.

It can also be helpful to use descriptive language to discuss feelings of attraction rather than to jump into labels and identity. This strategy shouldn't be used in a way that makes the teen angry if he or she has already embraced a gay identity; instead, it should be used to foster a less-emotional reaction from the parents, allowing them to stay calm and relate to their teen as a person rather than as a label.

When I last met with Jeremy and his parents, I had completed an evaluation around his behavior and concluded that he did not meet criteria for Gender Identity Disorder. In other words, he was within normal limits for what children do in terms of gender expression, although he did not fit into the narrow definition of masculine in his interests at his age. As I mentioned in the chapter, I worked with Jeremy's parents on their worries about homosexuality and what it would mean to them if he were to experience same-sex attraction later in life. They seemed to benefit from facing this possibility and finding ways to affirm their son and express unconditional love. They both wanted to be in a better position as parents to be helpful to Jeremy rather than sources of stress and anxiety.

MY ADULT CHILD ANNOUNCED A GAY IDENTITY: WHAT NOW?

In this chapter I introduced you to Mr. and Mrs. Sanchez, a couple who were genuinely distraught over their twenty-three-year-old daughter's recent announcement of a lesbian identity. The Sanchezes were stunned by this news and struggled to find the words to talk about it. Like many parents in these circumstances, they wondered if they had done something—or failed to do something, like keep their daughter out of competitive sports—that might have caused her homosexuality.

As with the previous chapter, if a person's adult child discloses a gay identity, I encourage them to stay calm and listen. I want parents to give themselves time to process and try to understand what their adult child is saying.

I also encourage parents to remember the three-tier distinction between same-sex attractions, a homosexual orientation, and a gay identity, so that they can use descriptive language to discuss feelings of attraction. Again, this provides them with some room to move around, to think about, and to relate to their loved one, and to keep from confusing the experience of attractions with the person and their identity.

It is important for parents to remember that their adult child has adopted a gay identity in large part based on what has become a recent and compelling gay script. Because there is no alternative script for them to consider, the choice is rather easy for them to make and often places them at odds with their parents, their home church, their understanding of God, and so on.

A significant issue that often comes up with adult children is that of limit-setting and boundaries. I encourage parents to keep in mind that limit-setting is symbolic, so it can be important to try to see limit-setting through their own eyes as well as the eyes of their adult child.

Given the strain that can be placed on a couple during this time, I encourage parents to attend to their marriage by turning toward one another rather than away from one another. Also, parents can quickly forget the importance of turning toward God, being honest with God by sharing with Him how they feel, including strong negative feelings like anger or confusion.

Mr. and Mrs. Sanchez found ways to be in a relationship with their daughter to the extent that they could in light of their convictions. For them, the relationship is much more limited than they would like, but it is realistic given the differences that exist. They have avoided becoming polarized as a couple. They also worked on identifying ways to take care of themselves as individuals and as a couple.

WHAT IF MY SPOUSE ANNOUNCES A GAY IDENTITY?

In chapter 7 we discussed mixed-orientation marriages, or marriages in which one partner experiences same-sex attraction or identifies as gay while the other partner is heterosexual. We talked about the general stages of relationship change: *awareness* (which is a time of either discovery or disclosure of same-sex attraction or behavior); *emotional response* (to the discovery/disclosure, which is often shock, confusion, disbelief, or anger); *acceptance of reality* (coming to terms with the discovered/disclosed attraction); and *negotiating a future* (deciding as individuals and as a couple about the future of the marriage).

Several suggestions were offered to the sexual minority spouse.

These included describing experiences rather than identifying with them ("I am a husband and father and I also experience attraction to the same sex"); exploring what attractions to the same sex mean (is it who you really are, or do your attractions reflect the fall, etc.); exploring what weight to give to other parts of who you are (e.g., biological sex, gender identity, intentions, values, etc.); and working toward congruence (aligning your behavior with your beliefs and values).

The challenges mixed-orientation couples face have been compared to interpersonal trauma and the challenges couples face following an extramarital affair (which sometimes, though not always, is a part of discovery/disclosure for mixed-orientation couples). It takes time to work through interpersonal trauma, and typically involves three stages: *impact* (initial realization of the effect of the offense), *a search for meaning* (coming to an understanding of what happened and why), and *recovery* (often characterized by better functioning following insight and moving past anger and pain; this is the time couples are in a better position to make a decision about the future of their marriage).

Sherri and James are still together and both have expressed commitment to working on their marriage. They have made significant changes in how they relate to one another and to the challenges James has been facing with same-sex attractions. He continues to gain insight into the patterns that have been a part of his life and is learning what it means to be more transparent and open with Sherri. James is a part of support groups that provide him with friendship, emotional encouragement, and accountability. For her part, Sherri is getting to the point where she can work on her reaction to the disclosure and find ways to process the hurt, anger, and loss, while finding ways to move closer to James as he shows himself trustworthy.

Jessica and Frank are also committed to staying together. Jessica made significant strides toward coming to terms with her attractions to the same sex while deciding not to pursue relationships. She instead has decided to invest in her marriage and family, a decision that reflects her personal and religious values. She deals with the loss that is associated with not meeting certain emotional and sexual desires with other women, and this can be difficult at times. Frank continues to be supportive of Jessica; he has been open to learning ways to meet more of her emotional needs. His openness has been encouraging to Jessica and seems to confirm for her that their decision to value their marriage is a good one.

WHOSE PEOPLE ARE WE TALKING ABOUT?

In part 3 of the book, "Questions for the Church," we turned our attention to two key questions that face the church community. The first was, Whose people are we talking about? I shared a story of an experience I had at a professional conference in which I finally understood how some people in the gay community saw Christians who were confused or distressed by their experiences of same-sex attraction. In some respects, it comes down to communities. Christians said they saw these sexually confused people as "our people," by which they meant that these confused people were part of the gay community, and Christians were concerned that they had somehow failed same-sex-attracted people.

It struck me that the church does not tend to see Christian sexual minorities as "our people"; rather, we see them as having more in common with the gay community than with the community of imperfect followers of Christ. The church has read from the gay script in a way that makes us expect and demand dramatic change of orientation, and this has kept the church from articulating an alternative script or preparing people to take a truly Christian approach to their sexuality.

Sexual minorities in the church—or believers who experience same-sex attraction—are *our people*. We have a responsibility to them that is not being fulfilled in the way the church is currently approaching the issues. I have found that framing the issue this way can lead to more compassion and resourcefulness as the church tries to identify ways to respond to people in the church who are sorting out sexual identity issues.

One distinction that may facilitate this is to recognize differences between what I refer to as "assertive advocates" and "sincere strugglers." Both are believers who experience same-sex attraction, but they approach the topic of homosexuality in different ways. Generally speaking, the assertive advocate hears negative messages from the church, has felt isolated for some time, and demands changes in church teaching that are quite radical. In contrast, the sincere struggler is trying to sort out how to live in light of their experiences of same-sex attraction. They do not want to change church policy, but they would like to find a church home, a safe place in which they can be more transparent about their experiences and struggles and find more practical support and encouragement.

My experience has been that the sincere struggler in particular has the potential to grow tremendously in his or her spiritual life, primarily because of what is gained in perseverance and character. This growth and spiritual maturity, over time, provides a basis for bringing light to the local church community.

WHAT IS THE CHURCH'S RESPONSE TO ENDURING CONDITIONS?

The last chapter answers the other question that I think the church needs to explore further: What is the church's response to enduring conditions? I introduced you to Terry and Linda, a couple with a unique story. If you recall, Terry struggled with same-sex attraction in a mixed-orientation marriage. Both he and his wife, Linda, are believers. Terry had had several same-sex relationships over the years, and eventually he contracted HIV. Over time, Linda came to forgive Terry, but she was also struggling with her own health concerns; she had been diagnosed with cancer.

I described how the church responded differently to these enduring or "besetting" conditions. Granted, Terry's HIV status was the result of his behavior, while his experiences of same-sex attraction were not. Linda's cancer was a different kind of concern. What they shared in common, though, were two besetting conditions.

Linda was able to share her struggle with her family, co-workers, girlfriends, church group, and others. She received tremendous support and encouragement. Terry has struggled in near isolation. Only a handful of people know about his attractions; fewer know about his HIV status.

I wanted to challenge the church to think about how we respond to homosexuality. Is it possible to learn from Terry and Linda and others who are sorting this out? Should we think about same-sex attraction as something that is more likely to be enduring rather than something that can be easily fixed? Based upon what we know so far about attempts to change sexual orientation, most people will not experience a 180-degree turnaround. Rather, they will experience various gains in terms of reduced same-sex attraction (for some) and an increase in attraction to the opposite sex or to a particular person (for a smaller number). Even in these cases, most people acknowledge that they still experience some same-sex attractions.

So if the enduring condition is same-sex attraction, how should the church respond? Generally speaking, in my experience the church can and often does respond well to other enduring conditions, but for some reason we struggle with same-sex attractions. The goal for the church should be to not set the expectations so high for those who are struggling in this area. We should support change attempts while not requiring change as a necessary step to a deep and mature spiritual life. In other words, the church needs to acknowledge that some, if not most, same-sex-attracted individuals will continue to struggle with this throughout their lives, yet that doesn't mean that they can't have a meaningful relationship with the Lord. Indeed, God's provision takes many different and unexpected forms.

What we can all do together in the church is become better stewards of all that God has given us. This will include our sexuality and sexual behavior. Some sexual minorities will do this by identifying as gay and Christian but transforming the connotations of the word *gay*, treating it as merely synonymous with the fact that they experience same-sex attractions. Others will dis-identify with a gay identity and form a primary identity around other aspects of themselves, including their identity "in Christ." But heterosexuals interested in the goal of getting others to identity in Christ would do well to lead by example rather than sending this out as one more message that applies only to sexual minorities but not to the rest of the Christian community.

Terry and Linda are committed to staying together. Terry continues to experience same-sex attraction, and he identifies ways to expand his social support while staying accountable to those closest to him. Linda says that she has forgiven Terry. Her cancer continues to be in remission, and she is open to finding ways to encourage and support Terry while they work as a couple on ways to grow closer to one another.

TWO FINAL WORDS

In conclusion, I hope you take from this book a sense of both *humility* and *charity*. Humility is necessary in how we approach our understanding of the causes of homosexuality. Since there are many different possible influencing factors, and no one factor appears to be the factor that determines sexual orientation, humility should move us away from placing blame on parents or focusing on simplistic explanations like the sin of "nothing-but-ism."

Charity is found in how we respond to those in our community who experience same-sex attraction. Fellow believers who are sorting this out are our people. We would do well to see them as our people, so at the very least we should always lead with charity. Charity is also found in realistic biblical hope. We can support efforts to change sexual orientation, but we can also make sure we communicate to our people that their walk with God, their spiritual maturity, their depth of character is not contingent on the degree of change of sexual orientation they experience. They can pursue a life in Christ, an identity that is central to who they are and is common with all believers. When each of us does this, we begin to taste some of our own future, some of what we are all moving toward as followers of Christ. Our purpose is to praise God, to savor God, to glorify God; *that* is the believer's essential orientation and identity.

RESOURCES

BOOKS

Alan Chambers, *Leaving Homosexuality: A Practical Guide for Men and Women Looking for a Way Out* (Eugene, OR: Harvest House, 2009).

Christine A. Colón and Bonnie E. Field, *Singled Out: Why Celibacy Must Be Reinvented in Today's Church* (Grand Rapids, MI: Brazos, 2009).

Stanton L. Jones and Brenna Jones, *How and When to Tell Your Kids about Sex: A Lifelong Approach to Shaping Your Child's Character*, 2nd ed. (Colorado Springs, CO: NavPress, 2007).

Stanton L. Jones and Mark A. Yarhouse, *Homosexuality: The Use of Scientific Research in the Church's Moral Debate* (Downers Grove, IL: InterVarsity Press, 2000).

Andrew Marin, *Love Is an Orientation: Elevating the Conversation with the Gay Community* (Downers Grove, IL: InterVarsity Press, 2009).

Lisa Graham McMinn, *Sexuality and Holy Longing: Embracing Intimacy in a Broken World* (San Francisco, CA: Jossey-Bass, 2004).

Douglas E. Rosenau, *A Celebration of Sex*, 2nd ed. (Nashville, TN: Thomas Nelson, 2002).

Dan O. Via and Robert A. J. Gagnon, *Homosexuality and the Bible: Two Views* (Minneapolis, MN: Fortress Press, 2003).

Lauren F. Winner, *Real Sex: The Naked Truth about Chastity* (Grand Rapids, MI: Brazos Press, 2005).

Mark A. Yarhouse and Lori A. Burkett, *Sexual Identity: A Guide to Living in the Time Between the Times* (Lanham, MD: University Press of America, 2003).

PAMPHLETS

Stanton L. Jones, *A Study Guide and Response to Mel White's What the Bible Says—and Doesn't Say—About Homosexuality* (Wheaton, IL: Wheaton College, 2006).

Mark A. Yarhouse, Stephanie K. Nowacki-Butzen, Trista L. Carr, and Christine H. Hull, *Sexual Identity: A Guide for Parents* (Virginia Beach, VA: Institute for the Study of Sexual Identity, 2007).

Mark A. Yarhouse, Trista L. Carr, Christine H. Hull, and Stephanie K. Nowacki-Butzen, *Sexual Identity: A Guide for Youth* (Virginia Beach, VA: Institute for the Study of Sexual Identity, 2007).

Mark A. Yarhouse, Christine H. Hull, Trista L. Carr, and Stephanie K. Nowacki-Butzen, *Sexual Identity: A Guide for Youth Pastors* (Virginia Beach, VA: Institute for the Study of Sexual Identity, 2007).

Mark A. Yarhouse, Jill L. Kays, Heather Poma, and Audrey Atkinson, *Sexual Identity: A Guide for Spouses* (Virginia Beach, VA: Institute for the Study of Sexual Identity, 2010).

WEB SITES

www.sexualidentityinstitute.org
www.sitframework.com

NOTES

CHAPTER ONE

1. This is Wesley's Quadrilateral. See R. G. Tuttle Jr., "The Wesleyan Tradition," in *Evangelical Dictionary of Theology*, ed. Walter A. Elwell (Grand Rapids, MI: Baker Books, 1984), 1116.

2. Milton J. Erickson, *Introducing Christian Doctrine*, 2nd ed. (Grand Rapids, MI: Baker Books, 2001), 68. Erickson goes on to say, "While detailed scientific descriptions or mathematically exact statements are not possible, inerrancy means that the Bible, when judged by the usage of its time, teaches the truth without any affirmations of error."

3. Ibid., 75.

4. The Old Testament scriptural passages that are commonly cited in the church discussions about homosexuality include Genesis 19:1–29; Leviticus 18:22; 20:13; and Judges 19. New Testament passages often cited include Romans 1:21–27; 1 Corinthians 6:9–11; and 1 Timothy 1:10. Biblical scholars also cite related topics, such as the Creation narrative (Genesis 1–3), Jesus' view of Mosaic Law (Matthew 5:17–18), and other passages. See Dan O. Via and Robert A. J. Gagnon, *Homosexuality and the Bible: Two Views* (Minneapolis, MN: Fortress Press, 2003).

5. Stanton L. Jones and Richard E. Butman, *Modern Psychothera-pies: A Comprehensive Christian Appraisal* (Downers Grove, IL: InterVarsity Press, 1991).

6. Lewis Smedes, *Sex for Christians*, rev. ed. (Grand Rapids, MI: Eerdmans, 1994). The instructional and pleasurable dimensions of sex are also discussed by Smedes.

7. For example, Song of Songs 4–5.

8. Neil Plantinga Jr., *Not the Way It's Supposed to Be: A Breviary of Sin* (Grand Rapids, MI: Eerdmans, 1995).

9. Mark R. McMinn, *Why Sin Matters* (Carol Stream, IL: Tyndale, 2004).

10. Plantinga, *Not the Way It's Supposed to Be: A Breviary of Sin*.

11. Smedes, *Sex for Christians*.

12. This is an interesting observation coming out of the research by David Kinnaman and Gabe Lyons, *Unchristian: What a New Generation Really Thinks About Christianity . . . and Why It Matters.* (Grand Rapids, MI: Baker Books, 2007), 41–60; 91–109.

13. John Frame, *Salvation Belongs to the Lord* (Phillipsburg, NJ: Presbyterian and Reformed, 2006), 311.

14. Rodney Clapp, *Families at the Crossroads: Beyond Traditional and Modern Options* (Downers Grove, IL: InterVarsity Press, 1993), 67.

15. Ibid., 67–68.

16. This section on Christian history is adapted from Mark A. Yarhouse and Stephanie K. Nowacki, "The Many Meanings of Marriage: Divergent Voices Seeking Common Ground," *The Family Journal* 15, no. 1 (2007): 1–10.

17. D. L. Carmody and J. Carmody, "Homosexuality and Roman

Catholicism," in *Homosexuality and World Religions,* ed. A. Swidler (Valley Forge, PA: Trinity Press International, 1993), 135–148.

18. Ibid; W. Lienemann, "Churches and Homosexuality: An Overview of Recent Official Church Statements on Sexual Orientation," *Ecumenical Review* 50, no. 1 (2004): 1–40.

19. L. L. Ibsen al Faruqi, "Marriage in Islam," *Journal of Ecumenical Studies* 22, no. 1 (1985): 55–68.

20. D. L. Carmody, "Marriage in Roman Catholicism," *Journal of Ecumenical Studies* 28, no. 40 (1985): 32.

21. Ibid., 33.

22. Those interested in an extended discussion of this are encouraged to read John F. Harvey, *The Truth About Homosexuality: The Cry of the Faithful* (San Francisco: Ignatius Press, 1996), 19–29; see also John F. Harvey, *The Homosexual Person: New Thinking in Pastoral Care* (San Francisco: Ignatius Press, 1987).

23. W. Yates, "The Protestant View of Marriage," *Journal of Ecumenical Studies* 22, no. 1 (1985): 41–81.

24. L. Granberg, "Theology of Marriage," in *Evangelical Dictionary of Theology,* 2nd ed., ed. W. A. Elwell (Grand Rapids, MI: Baker Books, 2007), 693–695.

25. Yates, "The Protestant View of Marriage."

26. Ibid.

27. Ibid.

28. Marvin Ellison, "Homosexuality and Protestantism," in *Homosexuality and World Religions,* ed. A. Swidler (Valley Forge, PA Trinity Press International, 1993), 149–179.

29. Stanton L. Jones and Mark A. Yarhouse, *Homosexuality: The Use of Scientific Research in the Church's Moral Debate* (Downers Grove, IL: InterVarsity Press, 2000).

30. Debate between Rev. John Spong and the Rt. Rev. John Howe at Virginia Protestant Episcopal Seminary, February 1992 (audiotape available from Truro Tape Ministries, 10520 Main St., Fairfax, VA 22030).

31. *Report of the Committee to Study Homosexuality to the General Council of Ministries of the United Methodist Church* (Dayton, OH: General Council on Ministries, 1991), 27–28.

32. George Edwards, *Gay/Lesbian Liberation: A Biblical Perspective* (New York: Pilgrim, 1984), 23.

33. The Roman Catholic Church's officially recognized group to assist homosexuals is called Courage. See http://couragerc.net/

34. Author's files.

CHAPTER TWO

1. Edward O. Laumann, John H. Gagnon, Robert T. Michael, and Stuart Michaels, *The Social Organization of Sexuality: Sexual Practices in the United States* (Chicago: University of Chicago Press, 1994).

2. In the more recent Hunter College Poll, questions centered on gay, lesbian, and bisexual identity labels rather than sexual orientation. See P. J. Egan, M. S. Edelman, and K. Sherrill, *Findings From the Hunter College Poll of Lesbians, Gays, and Bisexuals: New Discoveries About Identity, Political Attitudes, and Civic Engagement* (New York: The City University of New York, 2008).

3. Ritch C. Savin-Williams and Kenneth M. Cohen, "Homoerotic Development During Childhood and Adolescence," *Child and Adolescent Psychiatric Clinics of North America* 13, no. 3 (2004): 540.

4. Ibid., 539.

5. Ibid.

6. Ibid.

7. Ibid., 541.

8. Ibid.

9. Ibid., 540.

10. Mark A. Yarhouse and Erica S. N. Tan, *Sexual Identity Synthesis: Attributions, Meaning-Making, and the Search for Congruence* (Lantham, MD: University Press of America, 2004).

11. Savin-Williams and Cohen, "Homoerotic Development During Childhood and Adolescence."

12. Vivian Cass, "Homosexual Identity Formation: A Theoretical Model," *Journal of Homosexuality* 4 (1979): 219–235.

13. Lisa Diamond, *Sexual Fluidity: Understanding Women's Love and Desire* (Cambridge, MA: Harvard University Press, 2005). Label transitions included a switch to a lesbian label by 19 percent of participants; a switch to a bisexual label by 23 percent of participants; a switch to a heterosexual label by 21 percent of participants; and a switch to no label by 37 percent of participants.

14. Ritch C. Savin-Williams, *The New Gay Teenager* (Cambridge, MA: Harvard University Press, 2005).

15. Mark A. Yarhouse, Stephen P. Stratton, Janet B. Dean, and Heather L. Brooke, "Listening to Sexual Minorities on Christian College Campuses," *Journal of Psychology and Theology* 37, no. 2 (2009): 96–113.

16. See Yarhouse and Tan, *Sexual Identity Synthesis: Attributions, Meaning-Making and the Search for Congruence*; Mark A. Yarhouse, Erica S. N. Tan, and Lisa M. Pawlowski, "Sexual Identity Development and Synthesis Among LGB-Identified and LGB Dis-Identified Persons," *Journal of Psychology and Theology* 33, no. 1 (2005): 3–16. See also Michelle Wolkomir, *Be Not Deceived:*

The Sacred and Sexual Struggles of Gay and Ex-Gay Christian Men (New Brunswick, NJ: Rutgers University Press, 2006).

17. Note that the specific "identity in Christ" script takes on a particular form. It is possible to have other scripts and even other identity-in-Christ scripts that may say something very different to a young person about his or her faith and sexuality.

18. To borrow from Neil Plantinga and his book, *Not the Way It's Supposed to Be: A Breviary of Sin* (Grand Rapids, MI: Eerdmans, 1995).

19. This person is also a Christian, which underscores the earlier observation that a "gay Christian" identity could be derived from scripts—both "gay" scripts and "in Christ" scripts that have a very different meaning from the one I mentioned above.

20. Rogers M. Smith, *Stories of Peoplehood: The Politics and Morals of Political Membership* (New York: Cambridge University Press, 2003).

21. Dallas Willard, *The Divine Conspiracy: Rediscovering Our Hidden Life in God* (New York: HarperOne, 1998), 21.

CHAPTER THREE

1. Stanton L. Jones and Mark A. Yarhouse, *Homosexuality: The Use of Scientific Research in the Church's Moral Debate* (Downers Grove, IL: InterVarsity Press, 2000). My colleague, Stan Jones, recently updated some of this material in a journal article. See Stanton L. Jones and Alex W. Kwee, "Scientific Research, Homosexuality, and the Church's Moral Debate: An Update," *Journal of Psychology and Christianity* 24, no. 4 (2005): 304–326. This section is adapted in part from these previous reviews.

2. Simon LeVay, "A Difference in the Hypothalamic Structure Between Heterosexual and Homosexual Men," *Science* 253 (1991): 1034–1037.

3. J. Michael Bailey and Richard C. Pillard, "A Genetic Study of Male Sexual Orientation," *Archives of General Psychiatry* 48 (1991): 1081–1096.

4. They reported a 52 percent probandwise concordance rate for identical twins; a 22 percent probandwise concordance rate for fraternal twins; and a 9.2 percent probandwise concordance rate for nontwin brothers. See our discussion of probandwise concordance rates in Jones and Yarhouse, *Homosexuality: The Use of Scientific Research in the Church's Moral Debate*, 75–77.

5. This sample was drawn from the Australian twin registry, and the probandwise concordance fell from 52 percent to 20 percent for identical twins. J. M. Bailey, M. P. Dunne, and N. G. Martin, "Genetic and Environmental Influences on Sexual Orientation and Its Correlates in an Australian Twin Sample," *Journal of Personality and Social Psychology* 78, no. 3 (2000): 524–36.

6. For example, K. S. Kendler, L. M. Thornton, S. F. Gilman, and R. C. Kessler, "Sexual Orientation in a U.S. National Sample of Twin and Nontwin Sibling Pairs," *American Journal of Psychiatry* 157 (2000): 1843–46.

7. N. Långström, Q. Rahman, E. Carlström, and P. Lichtenstein, "Genetic and Environmental Effects on Same-Sex Sexual Behavior: A Population Study of Twins in Sweden," *Archives of Sexual Behavior* 39, no. 1 (2008): 75–80.

8. See R. Blanchard, "Review of Theory and Handedness, Birth Order, and Homosexuality in Men," *Laterality* 13 (2008): 51–70; R. Blanchard, J. M. Cantor, A. F. Bogaert, S. M. Breedlove, and L. Ellis, "Interaction of Fraternal Birth Order and Handedness in the Development of Male Homosexuality," *Hormones and Behavior* 49 (2006): 405–414.

9. Bearman and Bruckner found no support for either genetic influence on sexual orientation or the "older brother" effect suggested above. Rather, the only scenario that was statistically significant

was when an adolescent male who was a fraternal twin had a female twin sister (which more than doubled the occurrence of homosexuality). This effect was not present if the twins had an older brother, which the authors suggest may mean gender socialization could play a role in some forms of homosexuality. See P. S. Bearman, and H. Bruckner, "Opposite-Sex Twins and Adolescent Same-Sex Attraction," *American Journal of Sociology* 107 (2002):1179–1205.

10. This section is adapted from Mark A. Yarhouse and Jill L. Kays, "Homosexuality and Sexual Identity: An Update," in Doug Rosenau, Michael Sytsma, and Debra Taylor, eds., *Basic Issues in Sex Therapy*, pamphlet, 2008.

11. R. Blanchard, "Review of Theory and Handedness, Birth Order, and Homosexuality in Men," *Laterality* 13 (2008): 51–70; R. Blanchard, J. M. Cantor, A. F. Bogaert, S. M. Breedloe, and L. Ellis, "Interaction of Fraternal Birth Order and Handedness in the Development of Male Homosexuality," *Hormones and Behavior* 49 (2006): 405–414; R. Blanchard and R. A. Lippa, "Birth Order, Sibling Sex Ratio, Handedness, and Sexual Orientation of Male and Female Participants in a BBC Internet Research Project," *Archives of Sexual Behavior* 36 (2007): 163–176; A. F. Bogaert, R. Blanchard, and L. E. Crosthwait, "Interaction of Birth Order, Handedness, and Sexual Orientation in the Kinsey Interview Data," *Behavioral Neuroscience* 5 (2007): 845–853.

12. For example, one of the most recent studies on this theory found that there are degrees of handedness which further clarify the relationship. Having older brothers increased the odds of homosexuality in only moderate right-handed men. In both non-right-handed and extreme right-handed men, having older brothers had no effect or decreased the chance of homosexuality in men. See Bogaert, Blanchard, and Crosthwait, "Interaction of Birth Order, Handedness, and Sexual Orientation in the Kinsey Interview Data."

13. Charles E. Roselli, Kay Larkin, Jessica M. Schrunk, and Frederick Stormshak, "Sexual Partner Preference, Hypothalamic Morphology and Aromatase in Rams," *Physiology & Behavior* 83, no. 2 (2004): 233–245.

14. Demir and Dickson generated a gene fragment (the "fruitless [*fru*]" allele or one member of a pair of genes on a chromosome) that was spliced in either the male or female mode in the chromosome of the opposite sex. For example, if males are genetically manipulated, they will not engage in male courtship behavior. If females are genetically manipulated, they will engage in male courtship behavior.

    See E. Demir and B. J. Dickson, "Fruitless Splicing Specifies Male Courtship Behavior in Drosophilia," *Cell* 121 (2005): 785–794. What was ironic about an earlier study was that while genetically manipulated fruit flies also engage in "homosexual behavior," so did nongenetically manipulated flies—once they were put in the habitat with the genetically manipulated flies. This suggests an interesting twist about environment. See S. D. Zhang and W. F. Odenwald, "Misexpression of the White Gene Triggers Male-Male Courtship in Drosophilia," *Proceedings of the National Academy of Sciences USA* 92 (1995): 5525–9.

15. D. H. Hamer, S. Hu, V. L. Magnuson, N. Hu, and A. M. L. Pattatucci, "A Linkage Between DNA Markers on the X Chromosome and Male Sexual Orientation," *Science* 261 (1993): 320–326.

16. For example, brain imaging studies are also being conducted. Researchers have identified differences in brain symmetry and neural connections between homosexuals and heterosexuals that appear stronger for homosexual males than females. See I. Savic and P. Lindström, "PET and MRI Show Differences in Cerebral Asymmetry and Functional Connectivity Between Homo- and Heterosexual Subjects," *Proceedings of the National Academy of Sciences of the United States of America* (2008): 1–6.

17. N. E. Whitehead, "Strong Chance Factors in SSA," www.mygenes .co.nz/chance.htm (accessed April 23, 2008).

18. Ibid.

19. Warren Throckmorton and Gary Welton, "Multiple Paths to Sexuality: A Synopsis of Effect Size and Twin Research" (paper presentation, Sexual Identity Summit, Nashville, TN, September, 2007).

20. Adapted from Stanton L. Jones and Mark A. Yarhouse, *Homosexuality: The Use of Scientific Research in the Church's Moral Debate* (Downers Grove, IL: InterVarsity Press, 2000), 54.

21. I. Bieber, H. J. Dain, P. R. Dince, M. G. Drellich, H. G. Grand, R. H. Gundlach, M. W. Kremer, A. H. Rifkin, C. B. Wilbur, and T. B. Bieber, *Homosexuality: A Psychoanalytic Study of Male Homosexuals* (New York: Basic Books, 1962).

22. R. B. Evans, "Childhood Parental Relationships of Homosexual Men," *Journal of Consulting and Clinical Psychology* 33 (1969): 129–135.

23. Helen W. Wilson and Cathy Spatz Widom, "Does Physical Abuse, Sexual Abuse, or Neglect in Childhood Increase the Likelihood of Same-Sex Sexual Relationships and Cohabitation? A Prospective 30-Year Follow-Up," *Archives of Sexual Behavior* 39, no. 1 (2009): 63–74.

24. K. Alanko, P. Santtila, K. Witting, M. Varjonen, P. Jern, A. Johansson, B. von der Pahlen, and N. Kenneth Sandnabba, "Psychiatric Symptoms and Same-Sex Sexual Attraction and Behavior in Light of Childhood Gender Atypical Behavior and Parental Relationships," *Journal of Sex Research* 2 (2009):1–11.

25. E. O. Laumann, J. H. Gagnon, R. T. Michael, and S. Michaels, *The Social Organization of Sexuality: Sexual Practices in the United States* (Chicago: The University of Chicago Press, 1994).

26. William C. Holmes and Gail B. Slap, "Sexual Abuse of Boys: Definition, Prevalence, Correlates, Sequelae, and Management" *Journal of the American Medical Association* 280, no. 21 (1998): 1855–1862.

27. Stanton L. Jones and Mark A. Yarhouse, *Ex-gays? A Longitudinal Study of Religiously Mediated Change in Sexual Orientation* (Downers Grove, IL: InterVarsity Press, 2007), 164–165.

28. Ibid., 342.

29. Wilson and Widom, "Does Physical Abuse, Sexual Abuse, or Neglect in Childhood Increase the Likelihood of Same-Sex Sexual Relationships and Cohabitation? A Prospective 30-Year Follow-Up."

30. Judith Stacey and Timothy J. Biblarz, "(How) Does the Sexual Orientation of Parents Matter?" *American Sociological Review* 66, no. 2 (2001): 159–183.

31. David F. Greenberg, *The Construction of Homosexuality* (University of Chicago Press, 1990).

32. Percentages rose in urban areas as compared to rural: 9.2 percent (urban) versus 1.3 percent (rural) or 2.8 percent (general). The elevations were true for lesbians as well: 2.6 percent (urban) versus 1.4 percent (general) and <1 percent rural. Laumann, Gagnon, Michael, and Michaels, *The Social Organization of Sexuality: Sexual Practices in the United States*, 305–306.

33. Robert Gagnon, *The Bible and Homosexual Practice* (Nashville, TN: Abingdon Press, 2001), 416.

34. Laumann, Gagnon, Michael, and Michaels, *The Social Organization of Sexuality: Sexual Practices in the United States*, 308.

35. For example, Margaret Nichols presents the case of "Mike" and "Jenny," a couple in a nontraditional, polyamorous (open) relationship. After they worked through a number of issues not uncommon

in the polyamorous community, Mike worked on his capacity to respond sexually to other men: "More recently, Mike has become close with a bisexual man. Mike very much wants to have sex with this man, primarily because he feels it would enhance the relationship [with Jenny]. Although Mike is at most only incidentally attracted to men, he feels he can develop the ability to enjoy male-male sex because his sexuality is so flexible. Treatment interventions have included bibliotherapy and helping Mike identify ways he might find a 'tutor' in the gay male community." See Margaret Nichols, "Sexual Minorities," in *Principles and Practice of Sex Therapy,* 3rd ed. (New York: Guildford Press, 2000), 357.

36. "Answers to Your Questions about Sexual Orientation and Homosexuality," *American Psychological Association,* www.apa.org/topics/sorientation.html#whatcauses.

CHAPTER FOUR

1. "APA Task Force on Appropriate Therapeutic Responses to Sexual Orientation," *Report of the Task Force on Appropriate Therapeutic Responses to Sexual Orientation* (Washington, DC: American Psychological Association, 2009), 120.

2. Houston MacIntosh, "Attitudes and Experiences of Psychoanalysts," *Journal of the American Psychoanalytic Association* 42, no. 4 (1994): 1183–1207.

3. Readers familiar with this research will recognize that NARTH used the Kinsey scale to assess change in sexual orientation.

4. The one-year follow-up was of 140 people (from an original 248 the year before, of which 208 gave permission to be contacted for the follow-up).

5. Of the 200 persons, 143 were male and 57 female.

6. This does not necessarily mean that it is easier for males than females to experience change. What we see in this study is that a

higher percentage of men reported successful heterosexual functioning; this may reflect on more married men participating in the study or that men may be more likely to marry than women. This wasn't a statement about success but "good heterosexual functioning," which was measured by frequency of heterosexual sex, among other things.

7. Stanton L. Jones and Mark A. Yarhouse, *Ex-gays? A Longitudinal Study of Religiously Mediated Change in Sexual Orientation* (Downers Grove, IL: InterVarsity Press, 2007).

8. Personal interviews were conducted at Time 1; about 15 percent phone interviews at Time 2; and all phone interviews at Time 3.

9. Jones and Yarhouse, *Ex-gays? A Longitudinal Study of Religiously Mediated Change in Sexual Orientation.*

10. We reported results at the end of 6 to 7 years from 61 participants, having started with 98, so any discussion of percentages should take this into account so as not to be misleading.

11. "APA Task Force on Appropriate Therapeutic Responses to Sexual Orientation," *Report of the Task Force on Appropriate Therapeutic Responses to Sexual Orientation,* 53.

12. That is, 176 of 202, or 87 percent. However, it should be noted that this was a convenience sample and unlikely representative of those who seek change of sexual orientation given the way the study was conceptualized and the procedures for identifying those who failed in treatment.

13. That is, 26 participants or 13 percent of the sample.

14. Shidlo and Schroeder categorized eight participants as having made a successful heterosexual shift (and not struggling with it).

15. Lynde J. Nottebaum, Kim W. Schaeffer, Julie Rood, and Deborah Leffler, *Sexual Orientation—A Comparison Study* (unpublished manuscript).

16. Forty-three percent of males and 47 percent of females were "markedly" or "extremely" depressed *before* their change attempt.

17. One percent of males and 4 percent of females were "markedly" or "extremely" depressed *after* their change attempt.

CHAPTER FIVE

1. Concerning sexual orientation, Michael Bailey and Kenneth Zucker conducted an analysis of the research on the relationship between sex-typed behaviors and sexual orientation and concluded that "for both men and women, research has firmly established that homosexual subjects recall substantially more cross-sex-typed behavior in childhood than do heterosexual subjects." The mean effect size for men was 1.31, *SD* = 0.43; the mean effect size for women was 0.96, *SD* = 0.35. See J. M. Bailey and K. J. Zucker, "Childhood Sex-Typed Behavior and Sexual Orientation: A Conceptual Analysis and Quantitative Review," *Developmental Psychology* 31 (1995): 49.

2. See Kenneth Zucker and Susan Bradley, *Gender Identity Disorder and Psychosexual Problems in Children and Adolescents* (New York: The Guilford Press, 1995), 302–318.

3. For example, the official manual used by psychiatrists and psychologists to diagnose mental disorders states that "by late adolescence or adulthood, about three-quarters of boys who had a childhood history of Gender Identity Disorder report a homosexual or bisexual orientation." See American Psychiatric Association, *Diagnostic and Statistical Manual of Mental Disorders*, 4th ed. (Washington, DC: American Psychiatric Association, 1994), 536.

4. For example, in their study of white, black, Asian, and Latino male adolescents, Dube and Savin-Williams reported a range of awareness of same-sex attraction (8–11 years old), first same-sex behavior (12–15 years), labeling of oneself (15–18 years), disclosure of identity to others (17–19 years), and first same-sex relationship

(18–20 years). See E. M. Dube and R. C. Savin-Williams, "Sexual Identity Development Among Ethnic-Minority Male Youths," *Developmental Psychology* 35, no. 6 (1999): 1389–1398.

5. Mark A. Yarhouse, Stephen P. Stratton, Janet B. Dean, and Heather L. Brooke, "Listening to Sexual Minorities on Christian College Campuses," *Journal of Psychology and Theology* 37, no. 2 (2009): 103.

CHAPTER SIX

1. To expose themselves to revisionist arguments, parents can review Mel White's *What the Bible Says—and Doesn't Say—about Homosexuality* (www.soulforce.org/article/homosexuality-bible). Parents can also read *A Study Guide and Response to Mel White's What the Bible Says—and Doesn't Say—About Homosexuality* by Stanton L. Jones (www.wheaton.edu/CACE/resources/booklets/StanJones ResponsetoMelWhite.pdf). A thorough treatment of the biblical material can be found in Robert A. J. Gagnon's *The Bible and Homosexual Practice: Texts and Hermeneutics* (Nashville, TN: Abingdon Press, 2001).

2. John Gottman, *Seven Principles for Making Marriage Work* (New York: Three Rivers Press, 2000).

3. Jerry Sittser, *When God Doesn't Answer Your Prayer: Insights to Keep You Praying with Greater Faith and Deeper Hope* (Grand Rapids, MI: Zondervan, 2004); Philip Yancey, *Disappointment with God* (Grand Rapids, MI: Zondervan, 1997).

CHAPTER SEVEN

1. Adapted from Mark A. Yarhouse and Jill L. Kays, "The P.A.R.E. Model: A Framework for Working with Mixed Orientation Couples," *Journal of Psychology and Christianity* (2010).

2. A. P. Buxton, "Works in Progress: How Mixed-Orientation Couples Maintain Their Marriages After the Wives Come Out,"

Journal of Bisexuality 4 (2004): 76–82; B. C. Hernandez and C. M. Wilson, "Another Kind of Ambiguous Loss: Seventh-day Adventist Women in Mixed-Orientation Marriages," *Family Relations* 56 (2007): 185–195; J. D. Latham and G. D. White, "Coping with Homosexual Expression within Heterosexual Marriages: Five Case Studies," *Journal of Sex and Marital Therapy* 4 (1978): 198–212.

3. Kristina Coop Gordon, Donald H. Baucom, Douglas K. Snyder, D. C. Atkins, and A. Christensen, "Treating Affair Couples: Clinical Considerations and Initial Findings," *Journal of Cognitive Psychotherapy: An International Quarterly* 20 (2006): 375–392.

4. Kristina Coop Gordon and Donald H. Baucom, "Forgiveness and Marriage: Preliminary Support for a Measure Based on a Model of Recovery from a Marital Betrayal," *The American Journal of Family Therapy* 31 (2003): 179–199.

5. For an extended discussion of this research, see Jill L. Kays and Mark A. Yarhouse, "Resilient Factors in Mixed Orientation Couples: Current State of the Research," *American Journal of Family Therapy* 38 (2010): 1–10.

6. For an extended discussion of "Us" in marriage, and guidance on counseling through marriage conflicts, see James N. Sells and Mark A. Yarhouse, *Counseling Couples in Conflict* (Downers Grove, IL: InterVarsity Press, 2011).

CHAPTER EIGHT

1. For an excellent treatment of the topic of shame as it relates to sexual minorities, see Veronica R. F. Johnson, "Reducing Shame in Same-Sex Attracted Christians: A Group Therapy Intervention" (unpublished doctoral dissertation, Regent University, Virginia Beach, Virginia, 2009).

2. I want to thank Stan Jones for helping to make this distinction. Obviously, people cannot be reduced to categories that reflect one

of two groups, but it can be helpful to make a distinction that recognizes a difference between "strugglers" and "advocates" without making claims about the veracity of their faith commitments.

3. www.youtube.com/watch?v=TihG-ZHB61k (accessed May 5, 2009).

4. Mark A. Yarhouse, Stephen P. Stratton, Janet B. Dean, and Heather L. Brooke, "Listening to Sexual Minorities on Christian College Campuses," *Journal of Psychology and Theology* 37, no. 2 (2009): 103.

5. This is a point Alan Chambers has been making, and I point you to his book, *Leaving Homosexuality: A Practical Guide for Men and Women Looking for a Way Out* (Eugene, OR: Harvest House, 2009).

6. I want to recognize Richard E. Butman of Wheaton College for providing me with this language.

7. This section is adapted from Mark A. Yarhouse and Lori A. Burkett, "Living a Practical Theology of Sanctification," chapter 7 in *Sexual Identity: A Guide to Living in the Time Between the Times* (Lanham, MD: University Press of America, 2003), 108–111.

8. Stanton L. Jones, "Identity in Christ and Sexuality," in Timothy Bradshaw, ed., *Grace and Truth in the Secular Age* (Grand Rapids, MI: Eerdmans, 1998), 100.

9. C. S. Lewis, *The Weight of Glory* (New York: McMillan, 1965), 27.

10. Ibid., 28.

11. John Piper, "The Immeasurable Power of Grace" (plenary address given at the American Association of Christian Counselors' World Conference, Nashville, TN, September 16, 2009).

12. Dallas Willard, *The Divine Conspiracy: Rediscovering Our Hidden Life in God* (New York: HarperOne, 1998), 366.

13. Ibid.

14. Ibid.

15. Ibid.

16. Ibid., 348.

17. Ibid.

18. There is perhaps no good comparison to sexual orientation, and I am not suggesting it is equivalent to any of the conditions noted. To take less negative examples, some people are prone toward differences in personality, such as how agreeable they are (or are not) or how conscientious they are (or are not).

19. A good place to start is the book by Christine A. Colón and Bonnie E. Field, *Singled Out: Why Celibacy Must Be Reinvented in Today's Church* (Grand Rapids, MI: Brazos, 2009); see also Doug Rosenau and Michael Todd Wilson, *Soul Virgins: Redefining Single Sexuality* (Grand Rapids, MI: Baker Books, 2006).

20. Andrew Marin, *Love Is an Orientation: Elevating the Conversation with the Gay Community* (Downers Grove, IL: InterVarsity Press, 2009).

21. Ibid., 182.

22. Ibid., 183.

23. Ibid., 184.

24. Ibid., 185.

CHAPTER NINE

1. Letter from C. S. Lewis, in Sheldon Vanauken's *A Severe Mercy* (New York: Harper & Row, 1977), 146.

2. C. S. Lewis, *The Abolition of Man* (New York: MacMillan, 1947), 47–48.

3. Stanton L. Jones, *A Study Guide and Response to Mel White's What the Bible Says—and Doesn't Say—About Homosexuality* (Wheaton, IL: Wheaton College, 2006).

4. Lynne Truss, *Eats, Shoots & Leaves* (New York: Gotham Books, 2004), back cover.

5. Ibid.

6. My former pastor shared this illustration with me in discussing another topic, and I have adapted it with his permission for this discussion of sexual identity.